'This is a profound and searching book. C[...]
about it is its realism, even as it holds to th[...]
God. Charlie Cleverly scours the Bible an[...]
writers searching for wisdom on the central question of Christian
spirituality: How can we see God? This is a deeply honest book about
our longing for God and about the glimpses God gives us of himself.
Here is wisdom, intimacy, terror and joy. Above all here is love, for
God, for people, for the world, for the Church. What more can we
want from a passionate, faithful pastor and teacher who writes from
the heart?'

Rt Revd John Pritchard
Bishop of Oxford

'Charlie Cleverly leaves no stone unturned, no byway unexplored in
his urgent quest to discover the nature of God's self-revelation, and to
learn how, as it were, to put ourselves in the way of an epiphany from
God. This is a book for all followers whose spiritual vision has
dimmed, but it is also a book to revive those 'God callings' that
depend on such vision. How could the preaching and teaching, caring
and campaigning, prayer and meditation of the Church *not* be transformed through sharing this hunger for the face of God?'

Dr Geoffrey Stevenson
New College, The University of Edinburgh

'Since our world has forgotten how to be still and fills every silence
with meaningless noise and chatter, humanity has inevitably lost sight
of God. Charlie Cleverly has written an eloquent challenge to our
frenetic lifestyles and a passionate call to the human soul. This book
is a thrilling invitation to rediscover, in stillness and wonder, the presence of God burning in our hearts. It is a beautiful and timely call to
fall into the arms of our divine lover and to know, perhaps for the first
time ever, that we are truly loved. If the Church responded to the
profound message, heartfelt honesty, and deep yearning of this book,
there would be illumination and blessing in so many lives.

Murray Watts
Author, Playwright, Director

For Joanna Braithwaite
(1976–2011)
'Some people become part of who we are
and our lives are richer for it'

Epiphanies of the Ordinary

Encounters that change lives

CHARLIE CLEVERLY

HODDER

Unless indicated otherwise, Scripture quotations are taken from the Holy Bible, New International Version (Anglicised edition). Copyright © 1979, 1984, 2011 by Biblica (formerly International Bible Society). Used by permission. All rights reserved.

First published in Great Britain in 2012 by Hodder & Stoughton
An Hachette UK company

This paperback edition first published in 2013

2

A CIP catalogue record for this title
is available from the British Library

ISBN 978 1 444 70194 4
eBook ISBN 978 1 444 70193 7

Typeset in Adobe Garamond

Printed and bound in the UK by CPI Group (UK) Ltd, Croydon, CR0 4YY

Hodder & Stoughton policy is to use papers that are natural, renewable and recyclable products and made from wood grown in sustainable forests. The logging and manufacturing processes are expected to conform to the environmental regulations of the country of origin.

Hodder & Stoughton Ltd
338 Euston Road
London NW1 3BH

www.hodderfaith.com

CONTENTS

CONTENTS

Foreword

What is a classic book? For me it is one that stands out from the pile, one that you re-read, one that you recommend, one that you give as a gift and anticipate delight in the receiver. It is a book that makes me laugh out loud, or causes tears to fall down my cheeks, or forces me to put it down and pray or worship or confess; one that makes me utter involuntary gasps of delight at its insight. It is one which I find myself grateful for – one which I would love to have written myself. It is a book in which I learn about myself. A classic is a book that feels at the same time ancient and contemporary – that draws from the past, but opens up the future. One which reaches beyond its author's tradition or church family, one which I could give to the non-Christian or the Regius professor of theology, one which makes me a better person for having read it, one which fills me with a greater love for Christ. By all these criteria, Charlie Cleverly's new book qualifies as just such a classic.

How to describe this book? Spiritual theology, theological spirituality. It is poetry and theology, doxology and spirituality. Drawing on two millennia of church tradition and meditation, from Tertullian to Tozer to Teresa, *Epiphanies of the Ordinary* takes us on a guided meditation through the spiritual journey from birth to new birth, from life to death to eternal life. It is a walking with God along the valleys and mountain peaks of the Christian life – beautiful and painful, joyful and tearful, challenging and comforting. This journey of Christian discipleship is infused with rare moments when God stoops and stays for a while, closer than our breath, and discloses truth about himself or yourself. Charlie calls these Epiphanies of the Ordinary – they are moments of the extraordinary in the ordinary. Epiphanies turning the ordinary into the extraordinary.

In each carefully distilled chapter, Charlie presents to us a biblical cameo of one aspect of divine disclosure, and leads us in prayerful response. First, the presupposition of this book is that God is a God who by nature reveals himself, who discloses himself, who comes, and makes himself known. God is not distant, absent or indifferent. He is the God of epiphany, disclosure, unveiling, revelation. He does not play hide and seek. He seeks and finds and gives. He does not keep himself to himself, but in his very being is a self-giving God. The twentieth century Swiss theologian Karl Barth famously defined the Trinity as 'The self-unveiling [Jesus], imparted to men [Spirit], of the God who by nature cannot be unveiled [Father].' God in his triune essence is the unknown God who yet wills to make himself known to you. Pre-eminently he has done this through his Son Jesus, as Hebrews 1 says, but this same Jesus comes to us, by the Spirit and Scripture, in our epiphany on our journey. Secondly, this disclosure is given to his people, his church, his bride. As Emil Brunner wrote, this epiphany is 'revelation as encounter'. God comes to us in a speech act. This epiphany is not a signpost to the abstract, the metaphysical, and nor is it merely revelation as propositional truth. It is revelation as encounter, revelation as communion; in Martin Buber's terms, revelation as an 'I and Thou' – God as person meets us as persons, personally. The pre-eminent revelation of God the Father, through the Son, is mediated in encounter with the Spirit. Thirdly, this epiphany is not about information but intimacy. God gives himself to us freely, wanting us to give ourselves back to God freely. Doctrine may be formed to frame our speech and reflection on that epiphany of encounter, but they are no substitute for the encounter itself. Charlie Cleverly's book repeatedly draws us to respond to the wooing of the Spirit, into the lover's tryst with the God of love – as such it follows classic Augustinian theology, drawing on the language of love from the Song of Songs. Fourthly, epiphany, encounter, wherein God gives himself to us, causes the banks of our lives to burst, and the river of life to be poured into us to flow back to God in consecration, adoration and mission. Those who have been encountered by epiphany cannot remain the same, and they must go and live out this encounter in the world and be themselves a lesser epiphany of God to others.

This book is not easy, nor light. It is a deep place. It is a book to be read slowly, carefully, prayerfully. It took time to write, it will take time to read. It is a book to be savoured. This book is about divine epiphanies and I believe its reading will open your soul to your own epiphany with the Spirit of Christ through his Word.

Simon Ponsonby

Preface

I was standing in the kitchen with my wife Anita on a cold
October morning when the policeman arrived. He told us
that Joanna had been critically injured in a road accident.
Then within minutes, while still standing before us, he
received the message that she had died. I remember the
numbing sense of head-shaking refusal to take it in. We wept
and shook ourselves in disbelief and shock.

At thirty-four, Joanna was so full of life and laughter and
fun, as well as being packed with wisdom and encouragement and loyal faithfulness. She had been our assistant for
the past five years and was our friend and close ally. It was
Joanna who read the original draft of this book and enthused
throughout the process of writing. She was so positive that it
even steered me through the times of writer's block that inevitably accompany the process of bringing such a manuscript
to birth. And now, as the book went to press, she was gone.

Joanna was killed as a cement mixer lorry failed to see her
on her bike and drove over her. She was translated into glory.
She raced us to heaven. She who had so applauded the endeavour of capturing on paper ordinary epiphanies of an
extraordinary God was now involved in her own epiphany as
she found 'today she was with him in paradise'.

The next day I went to a mobile phone shop and needed
to re-boot my phone. 'We need your password', I was told. I

said the only person who knew it was my former assistant. 'Are you still on speaking terms?' asked the technician. How Anita and I wish that we could still be on speaking terms with Jo. We would ask her many things and enjoy her company. We would particularly ask how these epiphanies we had worked on for this book matched the real and permanent sight of the Glory of God in heaven. We would ask her how the Visions of Moses, Daniel, Ezekiel, John and others in history described in the pages that follow match what she is beholding now. But that conversation will have to wait. For the moment there is a far too wide chasm between us. One day we will go to her but she will not come to us.

I am grateful to the leaders, staff and whole community of St Aldates church who have been so tender, loving, thoughtful and faithful at this time. Above all, I am grateful to my wife Anita for her constant faithful companionship and sheer inspiration in the journey of writing about these 'Epiphanies of the Ordinary'.

But with this preface we both want to honour Joanna and dedicate this book to her memory. We treasure her life and everything about her. May her example as a laid down lover of God inspire many. And may this book about glimpses of what in the future we will permanently behold, be a comfort and hope to many.

Charlie Cleverly

PART I: COME

Come to me, all you who are weary and burdened, and
I will give you rest.
Matthew 11:28

Had I not been awake I would have missed it,

It came and went so unexpectedly
And almost it seemed dangerously . . .

A courier blast that there and then
Lapsed ordinary . . .
Seamus Heaney, 'Had I Not Been Awake'

epiphany [e*piph*a*ny]
From Greek *epiphainein* to manifest, formed as *epi*
– (forth) + phainein (shine) . . . Ecclesiastical Latin
epiphania. Middle English *epiphanie*.
1. A Christian festival observed on 6 January, in the
   Orthodox Church commemorating the baptism of
   Jesus and in the Western Church the manifestation of
   Jesus to the Gentiles in the persons of the Magi.
2. a) A manifestation of a divine being.

   b) Any sudden and important manifestation or realisation.
(Adapted from the *Shorter Oxford English Dictionary*, 2002)

It all begins with a vision. A Francis of Assisi or a John Wesley is gripped by a vision that will not let them go. But it is not a vision of what they're going to do. It is not a vision of a preferred future. It is not a vision of human activity. It is a vision of God, and how good he is, and how wonderful it is to be alive and a friend of such a Being.

Out of such a vision flows a desire to do good things for such a God. Then other people may gather, and people begin to pay more attention to what they are doing than the reality of God . . . At this point, the mission replaces the vision in people's consciousness. Once this happens, descent is inevitable.
John Ortberg, *Leadership Journal*

Open thou the crystal fountain
Whence the healing stream shall flow;
Let the fiery, cloudy pillar
Lead me all my journey through.
William Williams, 'Guide Me, O Thou Great Redeemer'

But we were eye-witnesses of his majesty.
2 Peter 1:16–19

CHAPTER ONE

Unveiling

This is a book about seeing God. It is a book about vision. It is about having your eyes opened in such a way that everything changes, forever, into a life of love. It is about epiphany moments that last a lifetime.

I am writing because my heart is weary. I like to think it is weary with well-doing, but maybe it is weary with religion. My soul is parched in a dry land where I don't find much water. And as I journey on, I find many who long for the peace that passes all understanding. We long for the Sabbath rest of quiet contemplation of the Christ. We don't easily find it in the noise of our activity. I believe I urgently need to move from activism to meditation and then eventually to encounter, from which flows that stream-of-living-water life. I believe that without seeing salvation I am a clanging gong or just noise. Without epiphany, I am only partly alive. I tread into a misty landscape, but I can't avoid it: without this I feel I may miss the Way. I must walk through the valleys of shadows if I am to find the route to the mountain-top. Or I may miss William Williams's 'crystal fountain' and die of thirst.

At the same time, I know that there are those who are given to behold the beauty of God, and this has been a recurring fascination of mine. It is an interest that I believe a postmodern generation, aware of the value of heart-experience, may connect to. G.K. Chesterton said: 'There is a road from the eye to the heart that does not go through the intellect.'[1] That classic of mysticism *The Cloud of Unknowing* speaks of 'destroying the ingenuity of our own learning and natural intelligence' as we are 'inwardly stirred by the Spirit of God'.[2] This may be an uncomfortable path, especially if you are based in a city like the one I live in, Oxford, where intellect is idolised. Yet intellect and intuition can stand side by side, granted equal value, provided we are seeking God's wisdom, which may shame the world's. God's wisdom invites us into seeing as well as into understanding.

In the Bible, that resplendent record of God's dealings with humankind, we are invited into a world where saints of old have truly 'seen' the divine. The stories are silent as to how exactly this works, but we can turn its pages and encounter different revelations of Christ's beauty. Before we climb up the Mount of Transfiguration at the end of this chapter, we shall glimpse him through the eyes of Ezekiel, as well as of Solomon before him, Daniel after him, and of John exiled on Patmos. If we begin with Moses, it is clear that God 'spoke with him face to face, as a man speaks to his friend'. The epiphanic glory of God was so present that it left his face glowing. But still he pressed in for more, saying: 'Now show me your glory.' He was rewarded, as we will see, with a timeless revelation of Love.

At the time of the golden age of Israel, David also claimed to have 'beheld him in the sanctuary', speaking of seeing God's power and glory.[3]

Apparently, as with Moses, this sighting prompted David to long for, thirst for, and earnestly seek him even more. It also prompted an outpouring of psalms on the theme of the covenant love of God.

At the dedication of the Temple (as had been the case at the dedication of the Tabernacle), those involved saw the cloud of the glory of God and fell to their faces. It is interesting that the understanding that accompanies this unveiling is to do with the utter 'goodness' of God. 'When all the Israelites saw . . . the glory of the LORD above the temple, they knelt on the pavement with their faces to the ground, and they worshipped and gave thanks to the LORD, saying, "He is good; his love endures forever." '4

Another who saw this cloud of the beauty of God was the prophet of the exile, Ezekiel. He takes trouble to describe in great detail what he sees,[5] beginning with 'an immense cloud with flashing lightning and surrounded by brilliant light'. He is one of the first to speak of seeing, within the cloud, 'a figure like that of a man'.

As Ezekiel sees, he is lost for words. He sees fire, brilliant light, flashing colours. His vision of the Son of Man is preceded by this amazing account:

> Spread out above the heads of the living creatures was what looked like an expanse, sparkling like ice, and awesome. Under the expanse their wings were stretched out one towards the other, and each had two wings covering its body. When the creatures moved, I heard the sound of their wings, like the roar of rushing waters, like the voice of the Almighty, like the tumult of an army. When they stood still, they lowered their wings.
>
> Then there came a voice from above the expanse over their heads as they stood with lowered wings. Above the expanse over their heads was what looked like a throne of sapphire, and high above on the throne was a figure like that of a man.[6]

There is loud noise, there are mysterious beings with wings, there is massive vaulted height sparkling like cut glass with a deep blue or purple colour. Ezekiel sees him on a throne of sapphire. He says that 'from what appeared to be his waist up he looked like glowing metal, as if full of fire, and that from there down he looked like fire; and brilliant light surrounded him'.[7]

He seems to be searching for the vocabulary to describe what he sees. In one of the most evocative and yet most tentative descriptions in the Bible, he concludes: 'Like the appearance of a rainbow in the clouds on a rainy day, so was the radiance around him. This was the appearance of the likeness of the glory of the LORD. When I saw it, I fell face down, and I heard the voice of one speaking.'[8]

The speaking and the hearing are important – but so is the seeing.

As we pause and take this in, we may marvel. Indeed, we might say that it was beholding all this that changed Ezekiel, just as it would a later seer, John, from prisoner into prophet. Sight matters.

We pause to ask: What is this capacity to see? Is there a discipline of intimacy, where a person trains their eyes to 'see in the dark'? Or is it an unveiling whose origins are solely in God's sovereign decision? I believe it is both. There is the divine decision. But there is also choice, and the plea to see (Moses' 'Now Lord, show me your glory'). As we shall explore later, some name this seeing 'contemplative prayer'. Others speak of Wisdom, or sudden understanding. Others call it mysticism. It demands a slowing down and a rooted atten-tiveness to God, but I would argue that it is common to those who knock on the door of heaven: as Jesus says, 'It will be opened to them.' We will return to the question of how this works in a later chapter.

For the present, let us observe that Daniel, another prophet in exile, prepared himself for inner revelation – achieved 'good eyesight', if you will – through a lifestyle that was courageous and counter-cultural. It involved fasting from fine foods and wines, against the wishes of his teacher. He avoided the rich foods of the court, and in that training ground which was effectively the Persian University of Babylon, he became, 'In every matter of wisdom and understanding about which the king questioned them . . . ten times better . . .'[9]

This challenge to stand out from the crowd for God's sake is a useful thought with which to entice Christian students today. I often pray, as I look out over the crowds of students in our church in Oxford: 'May God give us a new generation of political and administrative leaders in our lands who dare to be Daniels.'

Daniel is not only a brilliant administrator, but he also acquires this special eyesight. What he sees is similar to what Ezekiel before him and John after him saw. He sees thrones set in place, and the Ancient of Days taking his seat. He speaks of 'clothing white as snow; the hair . . . white like wool. His throne was flaming with fire, and its wheels were all ablaze.'[10]

Then, widening his gaze to include the future of all mankind, he sees: 'A river of fire was flowing, coming out from before him. Thousands upon thousands attended him; ten thousand times ten thousand stood before him. The court was seated, and the books were opened.'[11]

It seems that this special quality of 'seeing' accompanies Daniel through his influential life. Seeing is certainly a help to loving God truly, and without the experiential knowledge of the holy, we may remain weak. Daniel sees more than most. He sees 'one like a son of man, coming with the clouds of heaven. He approached the Ancient of Days and was led into his presence. He was given authority, glory and sovereign power; all peoples, nations and men of every language worshipped him. His dominion is an everlasting dominion that will not pass away, and his kingdom is one that will never be destroyed.'[12]

Daniel in fact sees the end of the world as all roads lead to Christ in eternity. 'He who has no vision of Eternity has no hold on time,' said Thomas Carlyle. Jonathan Swift said that 'vision is the art of seeing things invisible'. As mentioned earlier, this book explores moments of vision that have permanently changed lives, and sometimes changed the world. If we mention Paul, Constantine, Whitefield, Mother Teresa, Martin Luther King, to name but five, in each case we are dealing with epiphany visions of God, where the veil is drawn back and people see into heaven: the effect is to redirect lives forever.

De Quincey, in 1840, was the first to extend the meaning of epiphany to 'any revelation or insight'. He was the author of various tales, romances, biographical sketches, but also of the memoir *Confessions of an English Opium-Eater* (1821). It was James Joyce, a hundred years ago, who used the phrase 'Epiphanies of the Ordinary'. He meant a moment defined by 'suddenly seeing'. These moments were a spiritual realisation of truth. He believed that it was for the man of letters to record these epiphanies with extreme care, seeing that they themselves are the most delicate and evanescent of moments. He told a friend that even a town clock was capable of being an epiphany. 'It is only an item in the catalogue of Dublin's street furniture. Then all at once I see it and I know at once what it is: epiphany.'[13]

But before this, 'epiphany' meant to see a vision of God.

As we have already said, the Bible is packed with people who 'saw the Lord', or at least his likeness. These sightings are also called 'theophanies' (from a combination of *theos* and *phaino*, meaning 'God appearances'). It is my contention that these 'God sightings' in the Bible in fact define history, calling the people of God on to their next challenges. They spill over from the Bible into the history of the people of God. And I don't believe we need opium or any other drug to see them.

So it was that Paul 'saw a great light'; Constantine saw 'the Christ of God appear to him with the same sign which he had seen in the heavens'.[14] Augustine 'had in my heart infused the light of full certainty and all the gloom of doubt vanished away'. Ignatius 'saw clearly . . . the holy child Jesus, at the sight of which he received the most abundant consolation'.

John Bunyan 'saw with the eyes of my soul Jesus Christ was at God's right hand . . . O methought Christ! Christ! There was nothing but Christ before my eyes.' Jonathan Edwards 'had a view . . . of the glory of the Son of God . . . The person of Christ appeared with an excellency great enough to swallow up all thought and conception, which continued as near as I can judge, about an hour . . .' Whether this is a seeing with our eyesight, an inner understanding or some apprehension of God's presence, we shall explore later.

When Christ the desire of the nations came to earth, it was as if these glimpses of beauty earlier in the Bible, and since in history, stepped out of heaven into earth and John can truly say: 'We have seen his glory.'[15] Perhaps the definitive vision of Christ, of reality, of heaven touching earth is the unveiling of Christ himself at the event called the transfiguration.[16] As if being with him wasn't enough, halfway through the gospel story, Jesus is 'unveiled' (transfigured) and Peter, James and John see him in between heaven and earth, talking with Moses and Elijah. They want to build a monument, but a voice says: 'This is my Son, whom I have chosen; listen to him.'

I like to think that this affected all three of them forever. John ends up on Patmos seeing Jesus again in a vision on the Lord's Day. Peter writes of this in his epistle, saying that this moment shaped his whole life:

> We did not follow cleverly invented stories when we told you about the power and coming of our Lord Jesus Christ, but we were eye-witnesses of his majesty. For he received honour and glory from God the Father when the voice came to him from the Majestic Glory, saying, 'This is my Son, whom I love; with him I am well pleased.' We ourselves heard this voice that came from heaven when we were with him on the sacred mountain.'[17]

The third of them, James, was martyred and we do not know if this vision sustained him to go through that ultimate trial, but I like to think it did. Let us consider this epiphany moment and understand what it is that happens to these men who went from simply seeing to beholding and, in this beholding, were changed. We shall see that the key is to stop, to look and to listen.

Stop

This theophany vision of God called the transfiguration comes in a context of breaking away from the rush of life and getting away to quiet separation: we find them on a high mountain, having come apart from the crowds by themselves. They are not in Starbucks or some crowd of worshippers; they are alone in what Julian of Norwich evocatively calls a 'cloud of unknowing' – the cloudy, fiery pillar of the presence of God. A.W.

Tozer said: 'We must be still to know.' He wrote of the modern-day need for silence and solitude:

> Our fathers had much to say about stillness, and by still-ness they meant the absence of motion or the absence of noise or both. They felt they must be still for at least a part of the day or that day would be wasted. God can be known in the tumult of the world if his providence has for the time being placed us there, but he is known best in silence. So they held and so the Scriptures declare. Inward assurance comes from stillness. We must be still to know. There has hardly been another time in the history of the world when stillness was needed more than it is today; and there has surely not been another time when there was so little of it or it was so hard to find.[18]

Echoing this longing, Thomas Merton, writing at the same time but from a different tradition, issues a similar call to soli-tude. He wrote an entire book for contemporary culture, remembering the Desert Fathers, that group of third- and fourth-century leaders who – at the time of the legalisation and official establishment of Christianity under the Roman Empire – left the limelight and went into the desert in order to meet with God. 'Society was regarded [by the Desert Fathers] as a shipwreck from which each single individual man had to swim for his life . . . these were men who believed that to let oneself drift along, passively accepting the tenets and values of what they knew as society, was purely and simply a disaster.'[19]

And so today, to advance the cause of peace and destiny in our lives, we may need to retreat and find silent space before anything else. At any rate, Jesus, in order to help Peter, James and John to see, has to take them apart for a while so they might stop, look and listen. At the start of this exploration, we note the context of this first epiphany, this first sighting of God in all his glory – a context of prayer: 'About eight days after Jesus said this, he took Peter, John and James with him and went up onto a mountain to pray. As he was praying, the appearance of his face changed, and his clothes became as bright as a flash of lightning.'[20]

It is as they are praying that something happens – a big encouragement to us to press in to the place of quiet solitude and prayer, that we might 'see the Lord'.

Stop, look . . .

The sighting is tantalisingly brief, not giving us much to go on – but it is enough. Matthew tells us Jesus' face shone like the sun, and Mark tells us his clothes became dazzling white, whiter than anyone in the world could bleach them.[21]

This is a revelation about 'God, the blessed and only Ruler, the King of kings and Lord of lords, who alone is immortal and who lives in unapproachable light'.[22]

The same purity and brightness is common to all the visions and epiphanies we will look at. Another who saw such a thing was the brilliant composer, George Frederick Handel. Handel wrote his masterpiece, the *Messiah*, in just twenty-four days. He worked on his manuscript night and day, and hardly slept or ate. One day his servant opened the door to find Handel at his work with tears streaming down his face. Handel looked up and told him: 'I did think I did see all Heaven before me, and the Great God himself.' The vision he had seen yielded music that has inspired generations to faith in Christ. As Helen Keller, who gave her life to working among blind people, said: 'The most pathetic person in the world is someone who has sight but no vision.'

Something of this vision of the beauty of Christ has been caught by many through the centuries, even those we might regard as unlikely seers. Albert Einstein said: 'I am a Jew, but I am enthralled by the luminous figure of the Nazarene . . . No one can read the Gospels without feeling the actual presence of Jesus. His personality pulsates in every word. No myth is filled with such life.'

H.G. Wells may have glimpsed it when he said: 'I am a historian, I am not a believer, but I must confess as a historian that this penniless preacher from Nazareth is irrevocably the very centre of history. Jesus Christ is easily the most dominant figure in all history.'

If we take time to look carefully at this 'sighting' in the transfiguration, another thing we see is that Christ towers over history by the company he keeps: he has friendships with Moses and Elijah. Luke describes it as follows: 'Two men, Moses and Elijah, appeared in glorious splendour, talking with Jesus. They spoke about his departure, which he was about to bring to fulfilment at Jerusalem.'[23]

At first glance this conversation with Jesus about his 'departure' may seem practical. Something is coming up in Jerusalem. Maybe Elijah is remembering his own departure (2 Kings 2:11–12) and hearing Elisha crying out, 'My father! My father! The chariots and horsemen of Israel!' Who knows? Perhaps they are strengthening the Lord Jesus, since he is about to go through the agony of death. So it is that vision gives hope, gives courage, gives the capacity to continue – by giving fellowship, here apparently friendship, with those who have gone before.

The 'departure' of which they speak is, on a deeper level, Jesus' own 'Exodus', Christ's sacrificial death once for all on the cross, as he is going to bring to fulfilment even the demands of the Mosaic law and achieve ransom, redemption, adoption. Perhaps this is one of the reasons why God the Father interrupts the scene to say: 'This is my Son, my Beloved, in whom I am well pleased . . .' In other words: 'Wake up. There is about to be a sacrifice that changes the world forever.' Here, as elsewhere, epiphany can contain within it an awareness of the reality of the cross. When John, years later, sees heaven open, this is what he will see: 'After this I looked, and there before me was a door standing open in heaven . . . Then I saw a Lamb, looking as if it had been slain, standing in the centre of the throne . . . And they sang a new song: You are worthy to take the scroll and to open its seals, because you were slain, and with your blood you purchased men for God from every tribe and language and people and nation.'[24]

It seems when heaven opens and God shares his secrets, often what he wants to show us has to do with the manner of the dying of his Son. It is like a permanent picture on display in the entrance to the halls of heaven: 'The Departure'. The cross can be called the central event of history, alone having the power to reconcile man to God. Hence in heaven Christ bears the marks of his passion, and when the curtain into heaven is lifted, this is what people see. The glory of the sacrificed Christ is unveiled to John on Patmos and there is a hint of the powerful nature of his departure from this world at the transfiguration.

Stop, look, listen

The disciples stop and slow down to be alone with Christ – and so should we. They have an epiphany experience of seeing heaven open, and we may find we are granted this grace. Then they are told pretty bluntly to *Listen!* Again, this is something of a lost art today. The words of German martyr

Dietrich Bonhoeffer speak of this need as we begin a journey together:

> Many people are looking for an ear that will listen to them. They will not find it among Christians because these Christians are talking when they should be listening. But he who can no longer listen to his brother will soon be listening no longer to God either; he will be doing nothing but prattle in the presence of God too. This is the beginning of the death of the spiritual life, and in the end there is nothing left but spiritual chatter and clerical condescension arrayed in pious words. One who cannot listen long and patiently will presently be talking beside the point and be no longer really speaking to others, albeit he be not conscious of it. Anyone who thinks his time is too valuable to be spent keeping quiet will eventually have no time for God and his brother, but only himself and his own follies.[25]

What is it that is being talked about in this heavenly conversation at the Mount of Transfiguration? Apart from his departure and the cross, when we do get to listen in, the subject spoken of is sonship and love: Matthew records: 'This is my Son, whom I love; with him I am well pleased.'[26] Epiphany often, as we will see, speaks to us of a life of love. If we dwell on this and ponder, we will be led by the hand to see how God loves his Son, but also to learn about the love relationship he wants with us: listening, learning, loving. Peter is restrained from his natural response to the vision, his suggestion of 'building three booths'. In Peter's reaction, we sense the flesh, or religion, or expertise which wants to do something or to build something. Our first temptation in this mysterious field of 'unveiling' is often to do something that we can control; to be technicians of 'something useful'. But God wants us to do nothing except listen to his Son and to be in relationship with him. As Henri Nouwen says, commenting on this temptation for leaders today: 'The question is not: How many people take you seriously? How much are you going to accomplish? Can you show some results? But: are you in love with Jesus?'[27]

To dwell on those words again: 'Then a cloud appeared and enveloped them, and a voice came from the cloud: This is my Son, whom I love. Listen to him!'[28] We see in this moment a revelation that he is making clear the supremacy of his Son over Moses and Elijah. In addition and crucially: the Father loves Christ – he can't help it and he can't stop expressing his love. This tells of the uniqueness of the Son; it tells of the love of the Father for the Son; and then it draws us to love Christ ourselves. This love is contagious.

At the end of his life, Jesus prays that we might each have our own transfiguration – epiphany – moments; and that they would lead to this same love. This is what Jesus says:

Father, I want those you have given me to be with me where I am, and to see my glory, the glory you have given me because you loved me before the creation of the world. Righteous Father, though the world does not know you, I know you, and they know that you have sent me. I have made you known to them, and will continue to make you known in order that the love you have for me may be in them and that I myself may be in them.[29]

Jesus desires that the same love would be in us. He prays that we might be so filled with the Father's love for Christ that we have Christ in us indeed. How to get to this state of love, and live a long obedience in the same direction in it, is what lies at the heart of this book. So we turn now to this theme of discovering these shining moments in time, and learning from them. Our first enquiry will take us on a journey with wise men, who glimpse something and start travelling. They end up, as we will see, with their own definitive epiphany.

Collect for Unveiling

O God, who revealed the beauty of your countenance to your saints of old: grant us to buy from you ointment for our eyes, that we might behold you in the sanctuary to see your power and your glory and return to the love we had at first; through Jesus Christ our Lord. Amen.

Then felt I like some watcher of the skies
When a new planet swims into his ken;
Or like stout Cortez when with eagle eyes
He stared at the Pacific – and all his men
Looked at each other with a wild surmise –
Silent, upon a peak in Darien.
John Keats, 'On First Looking into Chapman's Homer'

We saw his star in the east and have come to worship him.
Matthew 2:2

CHAPTER TWO

Waiting: The Feast of Epiphany

Some years ago, our family moved to inner-city Paris for me to serve as a pastor in the French Reformed Church. On returning to our Parisian flat and our stimulating job after a Christmas break one year, my French assistant asked, 'Shall I buy some *galettes des Rois* for everybody on Sunday?' As an ignorant Brit I had no idea what she was talking about, but I soon found that in every supermarket in the land, in the early days of January, the shelves are piled with puff pastry cakes filled with almond cream (completely delicious if you pay a bit more money and buy one from a pâtisserie and not a supermarket). They may contain a little ornament, reminding you of the gifts of the three kings. For 6 January celebrates the appearing of Christ to the three kings. And indeed, because this is France, it is marked with a proper feast.

The way in which the Magi find their way to the manger, and the epiphany which follows, seem like parables for our times. The Magi are looking for truth. They are searching. And this book is for those who are searching. Our journey in this book will take us to investigate different epiphanies, different sightings of God through history – with the hope that as a result we may ourselves see him, know him, and live better lives.

These particular wise men are stargazers. They have been attentively watching the stars for years, and have no doubt experienced a eureka moment similar to that described by Keats in the lines above on the appearance of some new planet. Indeed, this is what these three see now: the star in the East, which was much longed for and changed everything. Wise men, astrologers, astronomers, weather-watchers; they see in a moment of deep darkness a new star – a new light, perhaps in the middle of hopelessness, and they decide to journey to see where it leads.

This book is an invitation to go on a journey. It is an invitation to epiphany. It comes from a lifelong hunger to press in – so far as such a thing is possible – to God, asking for more vision, more encounter. Jesus beckons to us: 'Ask! Seek! Knock!' is his simple invitation in all his teachings and parables on prayer. This book is an invitation to a daily asking. I hope to whet the appetite with every phrase. I hope to provoke a persistent knocking on heaven's door.

Jesus talks of searching for the lost coin, the pearl of great price. He tells of a widow crying out day and night for justice to a judge, a friend knocking on the door at dead of night for bread. These stories have in common hunger and longing for an answer. It is a hunger echoed in today's culture. Novelist Douglas Coupland, who invented the term Generation X, writes at the end of his compelling novel *Life after God*: 'My secret is that I need God – that I am sick and can no longer make it alone. I need God to help me give, because I no longer seem to be capable of giving; to help me be kind, as I no longer seem capable of kindness; to help me love, as I seem beyond being able to love.'[1]

Returning to the Magi, who perhaps also needed God, T.S. Eliot's poem 'The Journey of the Magi' has the evocative lines:

A cold coming we had of it,
Just the worst time of the year
For a journey, and such a long journey.

The poem is an account of the journey from the point of view of one of the Magi. It picks up what was for Eliot and is for many today a recurring theme of alienation and a feeling of powerlessness in a world that has changed because of the incarnation. The hopelessness is the angst of the human condition without God. Instead of a celebration of the wonders of their quest, the poem is largely a complaint – the journey was painful and tedious. The speaker goes on to talk about 'the voices singing in our ears, saying/That this was all folly'.

Many on this journey, towards epiphany and the new understanding it brings, will identify with this frustration as revelation comes in snatches. Yet in the end the wise man realises that the incarnation has changed everything. He asks finally: 'Were we led all that way for/Birth or Death?' The birth of the Christ was the death of the world of magic, astrology and paganism. The speaker, recalling his journey in old age, says that after that birth his world had died, and a new one had begun.

Some journeys, even those with worthwhile ends, are simply hard. Others journey more optimistically. Here is C.S. Lewis, in *The Magician's Nephew*, likewise describing a journey, though this one takes place in the sunlight:

It was a wonderful ride. The big snowy mountains rose above them in every direction. The valleys, far beneath them, were so green, and all the streams which tumbled down from the glaciers into the main river were so blue, that it was like flying over gigantic pieces of jewellery. They would have liked this part of the adventure to go on longer than it did. But quite soon they were all sniffing the air and saying: 'What is it?' and 'Did you smell something?' and 'Where's it coming from?' For a heavenly smell, warm and golden, as if from all the most delicious fruits and flowers of the world, was coming up to them from somewhere ahead.

'It's coming from that valley with a lake in it,' said Fledge.

'So it is,' said Digory. 'And look! There's a green hill at the far end of the lake and look how blue the water is.'

'It must be the Place,' said all three.[2]

This journey is also a quest – but it is undertaken in a far more positive spirit. Of course, this account comes from a book for children. But the fact is that some will find the journey to epiphany difficult and others will find it easy and joyful. Most will find there to be both seasons of winter and seasons of springtime in their life journey. This book attempts to consider and embrace both.

In the Bible account, what we know is that the journey takes the wise men to Herod's palace, where an investigation begins into where exactly old prophecies say the Messiah will be born. These, and the reappearance of the star, lead them to Bethlehem. They go in and offer their prophetic, meaning-laden gifts. For each gift the substance chosen hides a multi-level meaning: gold for a king, frankincense for a priest, myrrh for one destined to die. Crammed with meaning, these presents are suitable for an unforgettable moment. As they bow down, presumably they in turn see salvation in front of their very eyes. What is intriguing, though, is the mystery of the story – so much is left unsaid. I guess the baby himself is an epiphany of the ordinary: so normal an event, yet changing everything because of who the baby is.

The incarnation and the events around it: the arrival of Christ, the journey of the Magi, this first epiphany; all comprise an utterly unrepeatable event. But it is worth noting that new fathers or mothers, on first holding their child in their arms, are often aware of an epiphany of love. Often people will say they had no idea of the existence and depth of the wells of love within them that the arrival of their own child draws forth. Treasure the moment. Nourish and look after the well. It will not, God willing, run dry, even through the times of trauma that must surely come in every family. It only adds to the wonder when apparent outsiders – single friends, widows, lone grandparents – can experience this just as powerfully, as they are, like the wise men, ushered in to see.

Returning to the Magi, the stargazers, it is interesting that Jesus much later told his followers that in the same way that they knew how to look at and interpret the skies, they needed to learn how to interpret the signs of the times. Ordinary events are apparently to be watched carefully, with the same attention that those original watchers in the East paid.

Surprising though it may seem, in the Eastern Church, the Feast of Epiphany does not celebrate the journey of the Magi, but instead the story of Jesus' baptism. It is John's experience of the unveiling of Love that gets the name epiphany. And with this feast the custom is not the eating of cakes but the blessing of homes with water. With its different emphasis, the feast is also known as the theophany of Christ.[3] On theophany the priest will begin making the round of the parishioners' homes to bless them. He will pray in each home, and then go through the house, gardens and outside buildings, blessing them with theophany water.

A similar vulnerability to that of the Magi is captured in the testimony of John the Baptist. We may think of John as a hero figure who is out of the ordinary, and thus lose the reality of his humanity. But in chapter 1 of John's Gospel, we glimpse his real journey. Interestingly, the same intriguing combination of knowledge and uncertainty seen in the Magi appears again in the testimony of John the Baptist.

> The next day John saw Jesus coming towards him and said, 'Look, the Lamb of God, who takes away the sin of the world! This is the one I meant when I said, "A man who comes after me has surpassed me because he was before me." I myself did not know him, but the reason I came baptising with water was that he might be revealed to Israel.'[4]

John tells us the fundamental conflict of his life story. He says, 'I myself did not know him.' He is saying that he did not know the identity of the Messiah. He admits he did not know who Jesus was. John makes himself vulnerable. He shows the irony of his own story. He says, in effect: 'I was baptising people so that the Messiah would be recognised in Israel. And did I recognise him? No.' John admits to his ignorance. This is the unabridged version of his experience. Maybe he didn't know what he was looking out for. It is an ordinary story of ignorance and waiting, ending in extraordinary vision.

> Then John gave this testimony: 'I saw the Spirit come down from heaven as a dove and remain on him. I would not have known him, except that the one who sent me to baptise with water told me, "The man on whom you see the Spirit come down and remain is he who will baptise with the Holy Spirit." I have seen and I testify that this is the Son of God.'[5]

John tells anyone who is listening about his part in Jesus' baptism experience. He sees the Spirit come down 'like a dove' from heaven and remain on Jesus. Perhaps there is not language enough to describe what he sees; perhaps it does resolve into a fluttering presence like a dove. In this holy, sacred moment, time stands still and John takes a deep breath. He gets it: this is a time to be looking hard and paying attention. We can learn a lot from John.

We might think John, the one mentioned as a special child at the same time as the birth of Jesus, would always have known his calling to prepare the way for the Messiah. But it is as if he says: 'I had this incredible purpose but I couldn't apply it correctly. I didn't know who it was until the Spirit descended on this man I'd known all my life.' Even John, it seems, a man who had a promise on his life since before his birth, still struggles to 'see'.

Then he listens to the voice of the one who sent him to baptise in the first place. God speaks personally to John and gives him a full understanding about Jesus. And it's this voice that prompts John's testimony. This event is at the centre of his story. It would have been easy for John, the gospel writer, to narrate a purely positive story of the other John, the Baptist, to just portray the times when he knew and understood both his purpose and its outworking. But instead we are taken through John the Baptist's journey to epiphany. His path has involved long years in the desert. It has involved so much waiting. His example is a comfort and an inspiration to many in the desert place of 'waiting for the consolation of Israel' today. We too go through the not-knowing and then the knowing. The truth is that the waiting can last a lifetime, as it does for Simeon, whom we will consider at the end of this book. Let John's searching console us.

John's searching, in fact, continues even after this epiphany. Later, when the narrative has moved fully to the account of Jesus' life, John undergoes trouble even to the extent of being arrested and shut up in prison. In this darkness, he may have wondered: If I am the forerunner and cousin to the Saviour of the world, how can I be in prison? Am I mistaken after all? He sends messengers to Jesus who say: 'Are you the one who was to come, or should we expect someone else?' And then we read that Jesus 'replied to the messengers, "Go back and report to John what you have seen and heard: The blind receive sight, the lame walk, those who have leprosy are cured, the deaf hear, the dead are raised, and the good news is preached to the poor. Blessed is the man who does not fall away on account of me".[6] John's doubting is something he has in common with many. Incidentally, we must not confuse doubts and darkness with unbelief. Many travel though questions, and those who are wise put them to Christ, as John does.

Despite John's doubts, Jesus has no reticence about the role of John, it seems: 'This is the one about whom it is written: "I will send my messenger ahead of you, who will prepare your way before you." I tell you, among those born of women there is no one greater than John.'[7]

There was none born of woman so great, and yet even John had his doubts about his mission. His was a story steeped in miraculous prophecy and moments of epiphany – but also uncertainty and darkness. If this is true for John, the same is inevitably true for many lesser mortals today. If you ask about their journey and its epiphanies they will say, as people often do: 'It's a long story.'

In 2010, the BBC aired a new version of the gospel story, Tony Jordan's four-part series *The Nativity*. Jordan's own story is fascinating. He writes for the popular soap opera *EastEnders* and has been named number one television script-writer by UK magazine *Broadcast*. He has no religious background but found himself one day in a meeting discussing new projects. 'I initially pitched the idea of doing the inn in Bethlehem as a single play, a bit like the series *'Allo 'Allo*.'[8] This is the idea he was hired for but he writes that 'the more I thought about it, the more I thought my idea would be a travesty – to take the most beautiful story in the history of the world and turn it into a cheap gag'.

So Jordan began researching. He read the gospels. He read history books and consulted theologians – as well as NASA, in an effort to understand the star over Bethlehem. He says: 'I began to realise how little I knew about Mary or Joseph. It is about Joseph finding faith,' he explains simply. 'I had to ask the questions the audience would ask.' And through this personal research, it seems Tony Jordan had a conversion experience. When asked if he was ever tempted, writing the script in the wooden shed at the end of his garden, to dispense with the virgin birth, he says: 'If you accept that Jesus is the Son of God, why would you not believe that Mary was a virgin, and that God must have had some hand in the impregnation?'

He speaks about his discomfort with 'organised religion', as he calls it; with 'people who say to me if you come through these doors, walk down this aisle, sit on that wooden bench, and sing these hymns in this order, I have got God in a little bottle under my pulpit and I'll let you have a look'. He says, 'I don't think that was God's intention.'

He concludes his findings so far about Jesus: 'The only thing I know for sure is that the words I read as coming from Jesus Christ are the most truthful thing I have ever heard. As a blueprint for mankind, it is so smart that it couldn't ever have come from a clever philosopher.'

Tony Jordan is on a journey and his concerns about 'religion', as he calls it, seem less about Christ's body of believers and more to do with a wariness about accepting an easily packaged experience of Jesus in light of the distinctive nature of his own epiphany. He gives us a little window into his story. It is not too far from that of Jesus' cousin John, or even of those wise men long ago. May it encourage us to keep our eyes open, for our own sakes, and so that we don't miss the witness of people like Tony Jordan that – amidst uncertainty and apparent 'ordinariness' – epiphanies still happen that can change life forever.

John and the wise men guide our experience of the 'official' epiphanies, in that they are remembered each year by sections of the Church on that feast day. But the Bible is packed with more such, and so, I believe, is life. We now turn to one of the earliest, the 'sighting' given to Moses. We will see that it brings with it not only a revelation of God but a revelation of Love. As we turn the page, we can ourselves pray for revelation in the words of the ancient prayer that follows.

Cranmer's Collect for John the Baptist's Day
Almighty God, by whose providence thy servant John Baptist was wonderfully born and sent to prepare the way of thy Son our Saviour by preaching of penance, make us so to follow his doctrine and holy life that we may truly repent according to his preaching, and after his example constantly speak the truth, boldly. Amen.

Then her face lit up for a moment . . . For what stood in the doorway was Aslan himself, the Lion, the highest of all High Kings. And he was solid and real and warm and he let her kiss him and bury herself in his shining mane. And from the low, earthquake-like sound that came from inside him, Lucy even dared to think that he was purring.

'Oh, Aslan,' said she, 'it was kind of you to come.'

'I have been here all the time,' said he, 'but you have just made me visible.'

'Aslan!' said Lucy almost a little reproachfully. 'Don't make fun of me. As if anything *I* could do would make *you* visible!'

'It did,' said Aslan. 'Do you think I wouldn't obey my own rules?'

C.S. Lewis, *The Voyage of the Dawn Treader*

Now show me your glory . . .
Exodus 33:18

CHAPTER THREE

Seeing: Moses glimpses the Lord

The wise men travel to see the Christ-child; John strains his eyes and ears in the desert and in prison. But quite apart from these, before and after them, the Bible unveils successive visions of the glory of God. They seem to roll down through the ages; they are often accompanied by revelation of beauty and also of God's character or 'name'. Tragic Adam hides from the Lord God walking in the garden in the cool of the evening; faithful Abraham sees an angelic trinity of strangers by the oaks of Mamre. Exiled Moses sees God in a fiery bush and removes his shoes. Joshua opens his eyes and sees the commander of the armies of the Lord and, like Moses, discovers the very place he is standing, on the threshold of the Promised Land, is holy. The Bible story is indeed packed with people who 'saw the Lord', or some likeness, some representation of his glory. Epiphanies like those of Gideon, David, Solomon, Isaiah, Daniel, Ezekiel, Jeremiah, Joel, Micah, Habakkuk beckon to us. They may be said to define salvation history, calling the people of God on to their next challenge.

When Christ the desire of the nations came, it was as if these glimpses of beauty stepped down out of heaven into earth and 'we beheld his glory', as John says. I would say that almost every book of the Bible can be read as a story of a sighting.[1] Even Leviticus has more than one, where we read that 'the glory of the LORD appeared to all the people'[2] and the result was shouts of joy as well as reverence. Sometimes these unveilings are for individuals; sometimes, as here, the whole community gets a glimpse of God.

As is customary in God's dealings with us, we have to live with a paradox. There is a 'blessedness' in believing without seeing, as Jesus said to doubting Thomas. And yet we are invited nonetheless to see visions. There may be a 'dark night' at times. And yet the prophet Joel speaks of a Pentecostal age of the Spirit when young men will have as their real inheritance the seeing of visions, and old men will dream dreams. This must in part speak of revelation of the beauty of God.

It is fascinating that persistent Moses, despite several sightings, does not stop asking, 'Now Lord, show me your glory.' Different ages have different preoccupations. The deliberations of Augustine as to why Moses pressed God for this, and his conclusion: 'surely the answer is that he knew what he had seen was only physical and he was demanding a true spiritual vision of God'[3] may seem to us remote. For me what is impressive here is the persistent pressing into God for more vision, for more of a sight of him, for more revelation.

We need to press into God for more vision, more encounter. A.W. Tozer remarks:

At the heart of the Christian message is God Himself waiting for His redeemed children to push in to conscious awareness of His presence. That type of Christianity which happens now to be the vogue knows this presence only in theory. It fails to stress the Christian's privilege of present realization.

According to its teachings we are in the Presence of God positionally, and nothing is said about the need to experience that Presence actually. The fiery urge that drove men . . . is wholly missing.

Tozer was a man with a lifelong longing for God. Largely self-taught, he longed and laboured for the real thing, for the reality of the presence of God in the Church – but largely did not find it. He concludes this reflection thus: 'The present generation of Christians measures itself by this imperfect rule. Ignoble contentment takes the place of burning zeal. We are satisfied to rest in our judicial possessions and for the most part we bother ourselves very little about the absence of personal experience.'[4]

As we press in we realise clearly we are dealing with mystery. How was it that Isaiah 'saw the Lord'? How was it that John on Patmos turned around and saw someone 'like a son of man'? John was 'in the Spirit on the Lord's Day'. Isaiah was in the temple. Daniel fasted from the glutting food and drink he was offered because he hungered for God, and he was rewarded with nation-changing answers. This may encourage us to get into a place of seeking God's presence deeply in prayer both alone and with our community. At the same time, we are relying on the sovereignty of God, who will be found by whom he chooses.

Certainly, meditating on visions of God such as those mentioned above can help us and prepare our hearts. We begin with Moses' encounter with God recorded in Exodus 33 and 34.

We join Moses after the terrible disappointment of the golden calf. After forty days in the presence of God on the mountain, receiving the very oracles of God, he descends to disaster. If ever there was a time when a man might have given up, it was then. All the deliverances in Egypt and in the desert: the history of provision in Goshen, deliverance from the plagues, the survival of the first-born, the crossing of the Red Sea, the provision of water and manna and quail had not sufficed to separate a people for God. Moses must have felt discouragement and a sense of failure. He must have known loneliness, sick disappointment, blackness of spirit. And yet his exemplary reaction is not to step back but to step up and to climb into the presence of God. At times like this we see the utter greatness of the leadership of this meekest of all men on the face of the earth.

This is the haunting passage where Moses experiences seeing God 'with unveiled face':

> Now Moses used to take a tent and pitch it outside the camp some distance away, calling it the tent of meeting . . . And whenever Moses went out to the tent, all the people rose and stood at the entrances to their tents, watching Moses until he entered the tent. As Moses went into the tent, the pillar of cloud would come down and stay at the entrance, while the LORD spoke with Moses. Whenever the people saw the pillar of cloud standing at the entrance to the tent, they all stood and worshipped, each at the entrance to his tent. The LORD would speak to Moses face to face, as a man speaks with his friend. Then Moses would return to the camp, but his young assistant Joshua son of Nun did not leave the tent.[5]

Moses presses in to 'stand in the gap' on behalf of the people and we read that the cloud of the glory of God is around the place of meeting. Is this not what we should expect in the place of prayer? But even in that atmosphere, Moses still presses in. He has four prayers to pray – these could well be known as revival prayers. They are: 'Teach me your ways so I may know you'; 'Remember that this nation is your people'; 'If your Presence does not go with us, do not send us up from here' and, 'Now show me your glory.'[6] What instructive requests. So

instructive we will return to them in a later chapter. Suffice it
to say: here Moses is pressing on for the presence of God even
though he already knows it. He wants not simply God but to
know the ways of God that he might know him. He wants
God not simply in the place of prayer, but in society – calling
on God to remember that this people is his people. This is a
prayer to pray as we seek to unblock dry wells or 'rebuild altars'
in the redemptive history of our own nations. Third, Moses
wants transformation. He knows that the presence of God is
the answer for everything. Put another way, he wants the love
of God in the city and the community. But lastly, most impor-
tantly perhaps, he wants to see his glory.

How about you?

Moses is rewarded with a revelation, a vision, a 'sighting'.
It takes the form of the revealing of the character and nature
of God, the 'name' of God, that is a turning point for all
times. Moses hides himself in the cleft of the rock and all
God's glory passes by in front of him:

> Then the LORD came down in the cloud and stood there
> with him and proclaimed his name, the LORD. And he passed
> in front of Moses, proclaiming, 'The LORD, the LORD, the
> compassionate and gracious God, slow to anger, abounding
> in love and faithfulness, maintaining love to thousands, and
> forgiving wickedness, rebellion and sin. Yet he does not leave
> the guilty unpunished; he punishes the children and their
> children for the sin of the fathers to the third and fourth
> generation.'[7]

The last sentence speaks of 'tough love', justice and punishment: vital themes. But the weight of this vision or unveiling
is of unrelenting love. The passage in the Jewish rabbinic

tradition is said to reveal thirteen attributes of God, beginning with the first *Adonai* in verse 6, and ending with the
word *venakeh* in verse 7. The attributes are contained in the
verses as follows:

1 *Adonai* – compassion before man sins
2 *Adoni* – compassion after man has sinned
3 *El* – mighty in compassion to give to all creatures according to their need
4 *Rachum* – merciful, that mankind may not be distressed
5 *Chanun* – gracious if mankind is already in distress
6 *Erech appayim* – slow to anger
7 *Rav chesed* – abounding in mercy
8 *Emet* – truth
9 *Notzer chesed laalafim* – keeping mercy unto thousands
10 *Noseh avon* – forgiving iniquity
11 *Noseh peshah* – forgiving transgression
12 *Noseh chatah* – forgiving sin
13 *Venakeh* – and pardoning

At the heart of this revelation is the seventh expression, *Rav
chesed*. Its root word, *hesed*, translates as 'covenant love' or
'mercy'. The fact is that God is a God of love, and he loves
his people with inexhaustible benevolence. This is a truth
that we can count on, and can know experientially, and the
knowing of it will change our lives forever. Unlike the apparently random or anarchic gods of the Greeks and the unfeeling
deities of the stoics, the Judaeo-Christian God is abounding
in steadfast love *for you*! This is something that is hard to take
in but which can change everything when we do see it. It will
mean he is for you; and if he is for you, who can be against
you? Yet so few of us really manage to believe this, and hence

do not live life as lovers or loved. The result is a pale grey counterfeit Christianity that is sadly unconvincing.

However, when this truth is grasped, and by a community, the result is . . . revival. Or, one might say, it is in times of revival that this truth is grasped. We need to see the consequences of experiencing this covenant love, as well as uprooting the heavy slabs that may have blocked up its spring. But in history there are many testimonies to this revelation flooding the soul of men. Whether it is Luther feeling utterly reborn or Pascal's fire falling at midnight or Wesley's warmed heart or Finney's waves of liquid love, we can have confidence that this 'joy unspeakable' is there to be discovered – and we should not rest until we have it. Its consequences are, literally, life-changing. We will move from being fearful, edgy or rejected into a restful confidence that flows out in peace-dealing love for others.

Several major characters in the Bible grasp this *hesed* covenant love strongly. David evidently gets a revelation of it, as is seen in so many psalms proclaiming God's 'unfailing love'.[8] Solomon sings of it in the Song of Songs.[9] In this case it is a bridal, passionate love. Evidently Jesus lives it. One might say that the central message of Christ is to reveal the Father's love. Some have gone so far as to say that the central truth of the gospel story is when the Father leans over the battlement of heaven at Jesus' baptism, and at his transfiguration, with the words: 'This is my Son, whom I love; with him I am well pleased . . .'[10]

More often it is said that the central truth is the sacrifice of Christ at Calvary, where we find Christ's 'greater love . . . that a man lay down his life for his friends'. Here Father and Son together unite in an extraordinary act of combined love for planet Earth. God so loves the world that he gives his only

Son. In fact, all this is hinted at already in the epiphanic unveiling to Moses of the beauty and character of God. Indeed, where we read in Moses of God's 'tough love' – God by no means pardoning the guilty, but visiting sins on children – we can know that it will eventually be God himself who will bear the dreadful, just punishment in the person of his own Christ-child as *hesed* covenant love just carries on flowing from heaven to humankind.

It is in the light of Calvary that all this revelation of God's beauty and character comes to fulfilment. Let us pause to marvel, to worship if possible, this 'love come down', this 'compassionate and gracious God, slow to anger, abounding in love and faithfulness, maintaining love to thousands, and forgiving wickedness, rebellion and sin'.

Meditating on these attributes in the life of Christ, we see that at the start of his ministry, Jesus came up from the desert depending on his Father. His deeds were of 'compassion' for a people like sheep without a shepherd, compassion for the sick, the cancerous; compassion with backbone for the rich but lost rulers; compassion for the sexually caught-out-in-the-very-act. He was full of deeds redolent of 'gracious God', even transforming a village wedding from dry disaster to spectacular, vintage abundance. He rode on a donkey into Jerusalem, taking his time – but surely knew what he would find in the Temple: 'slow to anger'. Yet he was indeed angry when he saw the Temple authorities stealing, stopping access to heaven as a place of prayer, making his Father's house a den of thieves. He 'abounded in love and faithfulness', above all in going faithfully to his cross. Here he 'maintains forever love to thousands', millions, billions through history. In this great act, gazing from the cross, praying to his Father, he 'forgave wickedness, rebellion and sin'.

We must become people who see more. Moses had seen a fiery bush that was not consumed. He had known the holiness and power of God, as well as receiving his commission to lead a people. He had seen plagues sweep a nation at the word of the Lord, he had seen the parting of the Red Sea. He had seen the cloudy, fiery pillar – still he wanted to see more. He asks for a sight of the glory of the Lord.

I have recently been travelling on three continents. We saw many and varied sights: majestic mountains, spectacular ocean vistas, great ships, towering skyscrapers, forbidden cities, great walls, terracotta armies, and countless other breathtaking sights in China and Singapore, South Africa, and Europe. But the most important sight to see in this world is Christ.

Later we will explore the nature of spiritual sight, but, for the moment, we should notice that Moses is not concerned to ask for clarification: he asks simply to see. However far he has come, he knows that there is more. His life of calling begins and ends with a vision of God. The question I am asking myself is: Have I seen him?

Collect for Seeing

O God, who hid Moses in the rock to let your glory pass by before him, mercifully grant that we, being so sheltered in Christ, may have the grace to see also the height, length, depth and breadth of your love and to know that love, that we might live to give it away to others, through the merits of Jesus Christ. Amen.

> And truly, I reiterate . . . nothing's small!
> . . . Earth's crammed with heaven,
> And every common bush afire with God:
> But only he who sees, takes off his shoes . . .
> Elizabeth Barrett Browning, *Aurora Leigh*

I, John, your brother and companion in the suffering
and kingdom and patient endurance that are ours in
Jesus, was on the island of Patmos because of the word
of God and the testimony of Jesus . . . I turned around
to see the voice that was speaking to me. And when I
turned I saw . . .
Revelation 1:9, 12

CHAPTER FOUR

Continuing: John on Patmos

In some sections of the Western Church it is fashionable to think that prosperity indicates the summit of spirituality. In others, the decision to be a Christian is a choice to lose everything, and quite possibly die. The book of Revelation springs out of the latter. It opens with clear-sighted, obedient John who, far from enjoying a prosperous lifestyle and several international holidays each year, is bleakly described as a 'brother and companion in the suffering and kingdom and patient endurance that are ours in Jesus'. He is a companion of all who suffer, all who can't see, all who are dispossessed, all who have to endure. He is on the island of Patmos in exile, effectively imprisoned, because of the testimony of Jesus.

We might think his influence is over and his life is wasting away. But, as so often for God, the opposite of what seems naturally the case is actually true. John, in the place of prayer, is about to have a vision, a vision of the love of God and of God the lover, which by its inclusion in the canon of Scripture will speak to twenty centuries and more of seekers of God – and which still speaks to us today. Like his contemporary Paul in prison, or John Bunyan long after them, it is when seemingly most fettered that the gospel flies forth.

John is on an isolated island in a prison exile – like Nelson Mandela on Robben Island. He is cut off from his churches by a decree from unholy Rome, the current imperial power.

The gospel has apparently been a weak attempt to stand against unstoppable evil. Two generations after Pentecost, after the heights of Pentecost and Antioch, it is thoroughly discredited. Everything John believed and preached looks like a disaster. And then, unexpectedly, there is a monumental shift in this scene. This is no earthquake or political revolution – but something happens, and suddenly the prisoner is on his feet. He has a message. He has a job. He has a means of bringing God home to the people and the gospel to the world. The difference between John the prisoner and John the pastor is Christ: a vision of Christ and a true understanding of the reality behind the vision. This is a defining event that shows the transforming power of epiphany revelation.

John sees among the lampstands

someone 'like a son of man', dressed in a robe reaching down to his feet and with a golden sash around his chest. His head and hair were white like wool, as white as snow, and his eyes were like blazing fire. His feet were like bronze glowing in a furnace, and his voice was like the sound of rushing waters. In his right hand he held seven stars, and out of his mouth came a sharp double-edged sword. His face was like the sun shining in all its brilliance.'[1]

I pray often for a deeper understanding of this. It is for me a kind of 'eternal photograph' – one that changes lives. I love investigating the colourful, rich and dense imagery here. I don't feel this is fanciful. There is nothing more vital to believers than fully to discern the depths of God's personality. God will cause us to see his indescribable beauty, which in turn will focus our souls on the calling we have to make him known.

We are drawn to examine this picture in greater detail. He wears a golden sash, which denotes absolutely commanding royalty and governance. His head (where we would look for symbols of authority to rule) has hair that is white as snow, meaning age and absolute purity. He is the Ancient of Days. His eyes, like fire, speak of the ability to see or discern. They speak of his omniscience: a fiery knowledge that burns through our cover-ups, of bad motives, of the world's attempts to hide from him. His feet, like bronze glowing in the furnace, are a picture of his walk and the administration of his purposes as he steps out into all that he has planned. He is and has been able to go through absolute fire and come out glowing.

Next, his voice is like the sound of rushing waters. This is an utterly powerful voice, calling through the ages like Amos's roaring lion.[2] Of course, the Word of God is evoked: communications of truths coming from the lips of Christ rush down to us like an avalanche of water that will quench any and every thirst in the soul of humankind. His voice giving truths about redeeming love that keep on flowing through all the ages of man. He is the Word made flesh that calls a whole Church back to her first love, to putting first things first.

He holds seven stars in his hand. Then, as now, people read their star signs to try to catch hold of some astrological connection and meaning; here we see that Jesus holds all the stars in his hand for all time. A soldier with a sword in his right hand is ready to fight. Commenting on this passage, Eugene Peterson says: 'What is in my right hand is what I am ready to do and what I am capable of doing. What does Christ do? He runs the universe. It's as simple as that.'[3] The planets do not control us. Christ controls the planets.

'Out of his mouth comes a sharp . . . sword': this brings us back to his voice. Hebrews reminds us that 'the word of God is living and active. Sharper than any double-edged sword, it penetrates even to dividing soul and spirit, joints and marrow; it judges the thoughts and attitudes of the heart. Nothing in all creation is hidden from God's sight. Everything is uncovered and laid bare before the eyes of him to whom we must give account.'[4]

This text from Hebrews mixes imagery of eyes and voice in equal strength, pleading for attention to be given to the Word. The present age, I believe, is one where there seems sometimes a famine in terms of the Word of God. There are so many Bibles and yet there is so little reading, meditating, feeding. So little seeking of the manna, so rarely do we break open the bread contained therein. We live in an age of communication, texting, emailing, tweeting, blogging and Skyping – a seeming saturation with social networking, with more words flowing between us than ever before in the history of our planet. And yet, I believe we live in a famine of hearing, reading, meditating and eating the bread of life, the Word of God. May God save us – or our children – from being a biblically illiterate generation. Certainly one of the effects of seeing Jesus, falling in love with Christ, coming back to our first love, will be to love his Word, his two-edged sword.

I remember when first in love with Anita, who later agreed to become my wife, we lived in different countries for a year, long before the days of email. I remember how I waited daily for letters, and when one came I would save it up, smell the suggestion of perfume that had survived the postal service, then read and re-read it, devouring it until it became ragged. I would that a similar longing for the Word of God would be found in our generation and the next. David had this urgency

when he said: 'Oh, how I love your law!' For 176 verses of
Psalm 119 he cannot stop up his enthusiasm for simply the
words of God: 'To all perfection I see a limit; but your
commands are boundless. Oh, how I love your law! I meditate
on it all day long. Your commands make me wiser than my
enemies, for they are ever with me. I have more insight than
all my teachers, for I meditate on your statutes.'

Then what of the dear face of Jesus? When John sees this,
he perhaps thinks back to the day when he first put pen to
paper to attempt to describe the incarnation. Helped by
heaven, he wrote the prologue to John's Gospel: 'In him was
life, and that life was the light of men. The light shines in the
darkness, and the darkness has never put it out.'[5] This, for
me, opens up a powerful way of seeing him and his face, like
the sun shining in all its brilliance.

I believe John was hijacked out of his ministry and into
exile to show us the value of contemplation. Instead of doing
useful things, he is removed to a position of apparent irrelevance. He is in exile, ostensibly silenced. And yet it is here
that he can be brought back to his first love. Maybe some of
us modern activists would benefit from a season of immobil-
ity. Clearly prison is not to be desired, and yet some who
have been in prison have turned to contemplation and not
only enjoyed God but indeed changed the world: Paul, the
apostle John, John Bunyan; not forgetting those Chinese
believers of the last century, held for years on end, who have
courageously spoken of jail as a helpful training centre for the
Church in China. This is possible, I believe, if a leader is
prepared to move away from being addicted to approval or
addicted to being relevant, and move towards contemplative
prayer and a love affair with God. It may be that this is so on
the heart of God that he will permit such evil as detention for

his servants, knowing that it is not the worst thing that can happen to us – if only we use it well.

Henri Nouwen moved from the worldly relevance of teaching at Yale to the 'irrelevance' of working with the disabled at Trosly in northern France. He writes:

> To live a life that is not dominated by the desire to be relevant but is instead safely anchored in the knowledge of God's first love, we have to be mystics. A mystic is a person whose identity is deeply rooted in God's first love. If there is any focus that the Christian leader of the future will need it is the discipline of dwelling in the presence of the One who keeps asking: 'Do you love me?'

Nouwen expresses his view of what John is experiencing on Patmos when he is 'in the Spirit on the Lord's Day'. It is an epiphany contemplation of the beauty of Christ. Nouwen continues: 'Through contemplative prayer, we can keep ourselves from being pulled from one urgent issue to another and strangers to our own heart and to God's heart. Contemplative prayer keeps us home rooted and safe even when we are on the road, moving from place to place, and often surrounded by sounds of violence and war.'[6]

I believe this describes what is happening for John on Patmos and it can happen to us. John exiled is now John empowered – the vision did it. He is lifted from earth into heaven as simply a companion in suffering and kingdom and endurance – but he is put back as an empowered leader. The Spirit fills his eyes and ears with sights and sounds that will feed Christians ever after. It is not wishful thinking but real sight. A vision sees what is actually there, but on a different level. W.B. Yeats wrote:

'In dreams begin responsibility.' We might say: In visions are born realities.[7]

One key to seeing is to 'read, mark, learn and inwardly digest' the passages in Scripture where there are these epiphanies. For example, as we have seen, there are those of Moses, Joshua, Daniel, Isaiah, Ezekiel, David, Solomon, Zechariah, Malachi, Peter and Paul, to name but a handful. In addition we can be positioned attentively or, as John puts it, 'in the Spirit on the Lord's Day'. Having seen, we listen; having listened, we obey. Notably, we obey the Revelation call to 'come back to your first love'. Perhaps the key is to contemplate, to discover mystery or an unveiling that seems mystical. We will explore this more later.

Cranmer's Collect for the Second Sunday in Advent

Blessed Lord, who hast caused all holy Scriptures to be written for our learning, grant us that we may in such wise hear them, read, mark, learn, and inwardly digest them, that by patience, and comfort of thy holy Word, we may embrace and ever hold fast the blessed hope of everlasting life, which thou hast given us in our Saviour Jesus Christ. Amen.

How do I love thee? Let me count the ways.
I love thee to the depth and breadth and height
My soul can reach, when feeling out of sight
For the ends of Being and ideal Grace.
I love thee to the level of every day's
Most quiet need, by sun and candlelight.
I love thee freely, as men strive for Right;
I love thee purely, as they turn from Praise.
I love with a passion put to use
In my old griefs, and with my childhood's faith . . .
Elizabeth Barrett Browning, Sonnet 43 in *Sonnets from the Portuguese*

I Felt You And I Knew You Loved Me
Neon sign by Tracey Emin in Liverpool Cathedral

I will sing of the LORD's great love for ever;
with my mouth I will make your faithfulness known
through all generations.
Psalm 89:1

CHAPTER FIVE

Loving

I once asked my father what he felt the goal in one's life should be. He responded without hesitation: 'To love and be loved, old boy.' Later he gave me a present he had made for me. It was a calligraphy drawing of the words: *Ama et Fac Quod Vis*. I confess I had to ask him what it meant, and he told me it was Augustine's summary of the meaning of life: 'Love and do as you please.' He was not a particularly theological person and not really a churchgoer, but he had an eclectic recall for pithy quotations that stood him in good stead in every possible environment. I have kept this saying on my wall and pondered it for twenty years. It is in Latin and therefore mysterious and intriguing. But it is ordinary and banal in that it has been on my wall for so long I can forget about it. Yet it has been – or the idea behind it has been – a kind of epiphany: through it I see what matters.

This book is an exploration of stories of people who, in an 'epiphany revelation', have encountered Love that has changed their life forever. Likewise we think of those in history who had the veil of heaven torn back and 'saw' the beauty of the holy. Often they have gone on to a life of love, loving even when the waters of suffering are flooding in and seem to risk washing it all away.

Whether it's the twentieth century and the Beatles' 'All You Need Is Love'; or Augustine in the fifth century saying:

'Love and do as you please,' the number of those who define the meaning of life as finding and expressing love is striking. The following are typical:

'The greatest thing you'll ever learn is just to love and be loved in return.' (Eden Ahbez in his 1948 song, 'Nature Boy'.)

'The most important thing in life is to learn how to give out love, and to let it come in.' (Morrie Schwartz, *Tuesdays with Morrie*)

'Seize the moments of happiness, love and be loved! That is the only reality in the world.' (Leo Tolstoy, *War and Peace*)

Woody Allen deflates Tolstoy's bubble of seriousness, ostensibly agreeing but adding: 'Love is the answer, but while you're waiting for the answer, sex raises some pretty interesting questions.' There are genuine connections between spirituality and sexuality which we will explore. But it is love that defines the quality not only of our living, but even of our dying. 'At the evening of life, we shall be judged on our love,' said one medieval mystic.[1] Putting this another way: What would you like to be written on your tombstone? Perhaps it is advancing years that prompt this question to become more relevant to me, but I want to pose it to you now. Some suggest witty epitaphs such as Spike Milligan's 'I told you I was ill'. Others close to me have simply had their professions inscribed: 'Architect' or 'Farmer'. I heard of one that read: 'Father, brother, mentor, friend' – not bad, perhaps; but on reflection, an intimidating claim if not accompanied by love. Others, in this age when cremations are common, have nothing written at all apart from their name, for lack of space. What will you end up with? Answering this question can be a way of revealing your preoccupations in life.

For myself I have long since settled that I would like my epitaph to be recorded thus: 'He loved God and people'.

There are so many broken people looking for love and faithfulness that it seems a completely fulfilling aim. Sadly, I have
a way to go before this becomes completely true of me. Often
I trip up, or fall back to reactions of fear or control. But I
daily challenge myself to live up to this life focus. It may
seem a simple goal, but I have settled on it because I believe
it is the one thing needful, the one priority that matters in
this transitory life: being loving. I do not want to live like a
hamster racing round a wheel or a rabbit in a cage, or like a
cool but deadly snake. I want to live 'like a lover'.

For me, living a freely given life of love begins with being
a lover of God. Without this, love can become selfish or
beholden. With love for God truly breaking out into our
lives, and then ordering our other loves, love becomes true.

At the start of his defining work on this subject, *The Four
Loves*, C.S. Lewis flatly states: 'Every Christian would agree
that a man's spiritual health is exactly proportional to his
love for God.'[2] He goes on into the heart of this idea, arguing
that all loves can become distorted, bitter and dangerous
unless our love for God 'turns them into Charity'.

Many years ago, after a period of careful enquiry into
different spiritualities, I came to the conclusion that Christ is
irresistible and that the Christian story is intellectually irre-
futable. Initially reluctant, I just could not withstand the love
of God revealed in the face of Christ. His life, his teachings,
his courage, his truth and in the end his death and resurrection 'rang true'. That is not the subject of this book, and I
will not develop the argument here.[3] I mention it only to say
that I believe you will find, as I do, that if we want to grow in
love, it will help to catch a glimpse of the love of God first.

Those who have had this door-opening moment of revelation are longing to grow in their love relationship, we might

even say love affair, with God. They sense that it is from this love that love will flow for others. But even those who have at some point been blessed with an overwhelming encounter with the love of God may find that this love affair grows cold too easily. Like a fire whose wood flares but fails to catch light, their first love, which once burned bright, so quickly loses its heat. They find themselves weak when it comes to lighting the flame again, and so they go on living; but, in the words of Eliot, they are just 'living, living and partly living'.[4]

I am writing this book for those who realise that this is *the* life and death subject. Being a loving person, finding love for God and then keeping this love burning through the winter, and not letting the fire go out, is what I see as the key to everything: the pearl of great price. You might call it 'first love Christianity'; you could say it is a desire to love with a breaking heart. The fact is that few do love God today with heart, soul, mind and strength, and their faith tires accordingly. Despite our society's addiction to pleasure, the pleasures of loving God are rarely valued or even discovered by our contemporaries. Few even among the most 'spiritual' people are awash with love that spills over to all. Instead there is often strain and stress; and an over-commitment is common to many. In the end, one may be justified in asking: How does faith really make a difference?

When it comes to training for Christian ministry, passionate love apparently does not count: perhaps it is dismissed, or even categorised as 'enthusiasm'. My friend and colleague Simon Ponsonby once remarked to me that when he was interviewed for the ordained ministry, amid eighty or so hours of gruelling and thorough examination, Myers-Briggs personality-type analyses, academic enquiries and references, never once was he asked the question: 'Simon, do you love Jesus?'

And yet this is arguably the most important question today. Some years ago, A.W. Tozer wrote of what he called the 'missing jewel' of the Church. In *The Pursuit of God* (which could be a subtitle for this book), he said:

It is rare to find anyone aglow with personal love for Christ. This love, as a kind of moral fragrance, is ever detected on the garments of the saints. The list of fragrant saints is long. It includes men and women of every theological shade of theological thought within the bounds of orthodox Christian faith. This radiant love for Christ is, to my mind, the test of true catholicity, the one sure proof of membership of the Church Universal.[5]

My burden in writing this book is the desire that there might be a few more 'fragrant saints' around – and that that number might include you and me. I am writing to fan love into flame. I am writing to unblock wells of streaming love for God. I am writing to provoke and awaken love, which I believe to be the one thing needful. As we take this journey together, I encourage you to ask yourself if you are 'fragrant' with love for God. Are you a lover of God? Would your friends and peers describe you as 'One who loves God'? Is this what they would put on your epitaph? You may be ever so orthodox on all necessary points, or you may have doubts that you wrestle with daily, but have you learnt to love? Are you a lover? Do you live like one? Are your arms wide open? Or, like so many, have you grown weary? Have you learnt to protect yourself? Have you grown 'realistic', or even cynical? Has love grown cold?

We might ask: Is a love relationship with God so important? Surely people are more important? Of course they are important. But a moment's reflection shows us that love for God is paramount. It is important, first because he is worthy of love. Second, because to love him will have this effect on us and on others – it will refresh and restore and heal, and make all manner of things well. Without it we can become dependent and demand the love of others – which will never satisfy us. Only God satisfies. In addition, it is of utmost importance because it was so important to Christ.

When quizzed about the meaning of life – the 'command-ment of commandments', the *summum bonum*, the supreme good – Jesus cast his mind back and quoted Deuteronomy 6. These were vital words of summary, given as the people who had been slaves finally entered the Promised Land. After all the deliverances, all the wanderings and all the lessons of the wilderness, this was the deal desired by the lover of their souls: 'Love the Lord your God with all your heart and with all your soul and with all your strength and with all your mind.'[6] Jesus is saying effectively that this is still the thing to spend your strength, energy and life on. Only after this does he add the second commandment: 'Love your neighbour as yourself.'

It seems this love question was still on his mind when he met Peter after beating off the agony of death, asking him again and again: 'Do you love me?' Peter answered, 'Yes, Lord . . . you know that I love you,' to the point where he was hurt to be repeatedly asked the same thing.[7]

It was still on Christ's mind when speaking on Patmos to an exiled, patiently enduring apostle. John is our 'brother and companion in the suffering . . . and patient endurance'.[8] What happens to John is that he has a moment of epiphany that changes him from prisoner to pastor, from voiceless nobody to articulate prophet. He sees the heaven opened and the glory of God on display. But as I have already commented, the first thing the one with the eyes of fire saw was that the community at Ephesus had abandoned their first love.[9] He gently leads them back to what for him is an all-important lifestyle of 'first love'. It seems this is always on Christ's mind. The people in question were good at testing truth, at perseverance, enduring hardship, not growing weary. Yet Christ calls out to them about the one thing that mattered most to him: they had lost their love. Because of this, they risked losing everything. Was there already in those who received this message some strident religiosity, some coolness of feeling, because 'love', that greatest thing, had been lost?

Arguably the same was true for the Laodiceans in the next chapter of the book of Revelation, who were neither hot nor cold, who thought they had everything, but were, in fact, lukewarm; had nothing. They apparently made Christ sick.

And how about me – how about us? Do we too make him sick; or have we kept love alive? Despite the pressure and strain of modern living, are we living like a lover? And if not, then how can we discover, recover and maintain love?

In the call of the book of Revelation to come back to our first love lies also the first key as to how to do so. For Revelation is so titled because it is a 'revealing', a vision of the beauty of Christ. I would say first of all that love begins with a vision.

This is true of the love affair between a man and a woman. Often it starts with a vision of loveliness or beauty of the other. It may, though, be a progressive revelation as attributes are admired which then give way to a metaphorical 'catching sight for the first time' of the other as a thing of beauty and admiration. In the same way, love for God must begin with a vision of the beauty of God.

Moses keeps on asking of God: 'Show me your glory.' He is rewarded with a sight of the character and hence the majesty of God. I recommend his prayer: 'Show me your glory.' In Moses' case it was rewarded with a revelation of 'The LORD, the LORD . . . abounding in love and faithfulness . . .'[10]

We turn now to consider what happens when we contemplate that love.

Collect for Loving

O God, who taught us in your Son a strong, hearty, mindful, sacrificial love that sets our souls and bodies free: mercifully grant that we be given to see you and love you with our whole heart, mind, soul and strength, and then our neighbour as ourselves; through Jesus Christ our Lord. Amen.

If there is any focus that the Christian leader of the future will need, it is the discipline of dwelling in the presence of the One who keeps asking us: 'Do you love me?' . . . This is the discipline of contemplative prayer. Through contemplative prayer, we can keep ourselves from being pulled from one urgent issue to another and from becoming strangers to our own heart and to God's heart. Contemplative prayer keeps us home, rooted and safe, even when we are on the road.

Henry J. M. Nouwen, *In the Name of Jesus*

Father, I want those you have given me to be with me where I am, and to see my glory.

John 17:24

CHAPTER SIX

Contemplating

Twenty years ago, when moving with my family to France, where we lived for ten years, I came across the writings and heard the story of Catholic priest and writer Henri Nouwen. His story is challenging and prophetic in the city and seat-of-learning where I serve, Oxford. Henri taught pastoral psychology and theology for twenty years at Harvard before experiencing what he called a 'deep inner threat' as he found that growing older did not necessarily bring him closer to Jesus. Instead he felt close to burnout, which he called 'a convenient term for spiritual death'. He concluded that 'the question is not: How many people take you seriously? How much are you going to accomplish? Can you show me some results? But: are you in love with Jesus? Perhaps another way of putting it is: Do you know the incarnate God?' Nouwen pleads for contemplation, which he calls moving away from 'the temptation to be relevant' and towards a conscious irrelevance which breaks with the worldly addictions to success and driven-ness. Nouwen lived this out as he moved from among the best and the brightest at Harvard to live in a community of people with disabilities in a forgotten corner of northern France.

At the same time as hearing a call to love Christ, he also heard his call to 'feed his lambs', i.e. to love people. He continues: 'In our world of loneliness and despair, there is an enormous need for men and women who know the heart of God, a heart that forgives, cares and reaches out and wants to heal . . . In that heart there is no suspicion, no vindictiveness, no resentment . . .'[1] These twin calls were put together by Christ in the great commandment to love God and neighbour, and often come together: a vision of the love of God leading to a life of laid-down love for people. We might say: what God has joined together, let not man divide. Yet to 'see God' may be difficult in our age of bustle and rush and important projects. What is needed is a slowing down and waking up to mystery.

German Jesuit Karl Rahner famously said: 'The devout Christian of the future will either be a "mystic" . . . or he will cease to be anything at all.' This rings true for many. Franciscan writer Richard Rohr quotes Rahner and goes on to say that

> the great mystics invite us to know better, to draw from the resources of our own tradition and see in a way that honours debate, reason and order while also moving beyond them. Can we answer the great mystics' invitation? Can we begin to attain the great mystical gaze as Rahner says we must? I think we are on the very edge of history – and about to be edged over – by the depth of need and by the depths of our own desire.'[2]

Rohr speaks into the parched lands of many in articulating this. Yet this longing for God is a common thread through history. A.W. Tozer puts it like this at the start of his classic *The Pursuit of God*: 'Come near to the holy men and women of the past and you will soon feel the heat of their desire after God. They mourned for Him, they prayed and wrestled and sought for Him day and night, in season and out, and when they had found Him the finding was all the sweeter for the long seeking.' Tozer goes on to talk of Moses' urgency for God – but there are so many he could have chosen.

We find this hunger in Spurgeon and in John Wesley, in Charles Finney and in so many who have pursued God tirelessly. George Whitefield, forerunner of the Great Awakening in the eighteenth century, testifies that: 'If the trees of a certain wood near Stonehouse could speak they would tell what wonderful communion . . . I enjoyed with our blessed God there. Sometimes as I was walking my soul would make such leaps that it would almost go out of the body . . . At other times I would be . . . overpowered by a sense of God's infinite majesty.'[3]

In a sermon given in 1843, Charles Finney, American lawyer turned great persuader and preacher, said this:

> Nothing can make us stable Christians but to behold his glory, a revelation of Him to us. No excitement, no intellectual acumen, no strength of logic, nothing can secure us but a revelation of God to our souls. We should therefore persevere and insist that this be done for us, that we see God's glory, and be fixed on Him. The church should pray for ministers and for candidates for the ministry, that God would reveal to them the deep secrets of His love and mercy; that He would open to them the ever-flowing fountains of exquisite and perennial blessedness to let them drink from there and never thirst more.

He goes on to exhort churches to 'feel how much they can do for their ministers, by praying the heavens open, and letting down on their hearts such rays of glory . . . as that the spirit of the Highest shall come upon them, and the power of God overshadow them, and transform them from men of clay, to angels of mercy and power to a fallen world'.[4]

No doubt we should pray in the same way today. It is an ancient cry that Finney is giving – it echoes the words of Christ himself to the lukewarm Laodicean church. Finney is longing for men of clay to awaken. But to do so, they may need to stop completely still and know God, in order to then start running again.

'We must be still to know' is another phrase of A.W. Tozer's that calls out to our age of activity and noise and relentless networking. The lukewarm, neither-one-thing-nor-the-other church in Laodicea were counselled by the risen Christ to buy eye-salve so that they might see. So is there some kind of ointment that we can somehow get hold of? I believe that there is, but that perhaps it will cost us dear. It will cost us our ceaseless activity and apparent relevance and remove us to the desert of quiet waiting in the place of contemplation. I wonder sometimes if I am as ready for that as I know I need to be.

Two disciplines of intimacy are to be recommended in this quest for a lifestyle open to epiphany: meditation and contemplation. To be more specific, biblical meditation and contemplative prayer. They are two sides of the same coin, and are very valuable currency. Christian meditation is a rich heritage which, in a sense, any preacher must almost inevitably explore as they prepare to preach on a passage of Scripture. But it can be used as a daily discipline, if only we will give it time. It can be discovered through Ignatius Loyola's 'Exercises', where one enters a biblical scene and uses one's imagination to see, hear, smell and encounter the living Word, and thus be equipped for the day to come. Teresa of Avila defined meditation as follows: 'By meditation I mean prolonged reasoning with the understanding, in this way. We begin by thinking of the favour which God bestowed on us by giving his only son; and we do not stop there, but proceed to consider the mysteries of his whole glorious life.'[5]

So Christian meditation contrasts radically with much Eastern meditation, which has to do with emptying oneself and with the use of repeated mantras. Instead, we are concerned to fill our mind with biblical truth and to heighten personal relationships with the Father through the Son.

The word meditation comes from the Latin *meditare*, which means to consider or contemplate. It leads us to explore contemplation. Like all prayer, contemplative prayer needs to be rooted in biblical truth. It must match the Maker's instructions and the advice of Christ. Like meditation, it works best when gazing at the scenes or truths or words of the Bible. Contemplatives like to think of three basic steps towards the presence of God. The first is 'Recollection'.[6] It simply means to re-collect ourselves, putting away obstacles and distractions in the heart. We allow Christ to say to the storms of our heart, 'Peace: be still.' The truth is that this is far from easy: our flesh will complain loudly at being neglected. We may feel anxiety rising at all the things we need to be getting on with. If at first we achieve no more than an understanding of how much we lack inner unity, then something is achieved. We are leaning and looking towards the One who is our peace.

The second step is what Teresa of Avila called 'the prayer of quiet'. Stillness, but a listening stillness. We are alert and awakened, as if on tiptoes in our spirit, to *listen*. We respond to the transfiguration instruction about God's Son whom he loves: to *listen* to him.

François Fénelon says: 'Be silent, and listen to God. Let your heart be in such a state of preparation that his spirit may impress upon you such virtues as will please him. The silence of all outward and earthly affections and thoughts is essential if we are to hear his voice.'[7] John of the Cross uses the graphic phrase 'my house now all being stilled' for the moment to go out into the night to meet the Beloved.

The final step is into what Hudson Taylor calls 'Union and Communion'.[8] Others call this, for want of a better phrase, spiritual ecstasy. This is something we can dimly apprehend and is not for us to make happen ourselves – it is God's visitation. Julian of Norwich says: 'The whole reason we pray is to be united into the vision and contemplation of him to whom we pray.' Madame Guyon writes: 'We now come to the ultimate stage of Christian experience: Divine Union. This cannot be brought about merely by your own experience. Meditation will not bring divine union; neither will love, nor worship, nor your devotion, nor your sacrifice . . . Eventually it will take an *act of God* to make union a reality.'[9]

Yet Jesus promises that this can be possible. He calls us to 'Abide in me as I abide in you' and he prays that we might be one in him. Richard Foster has a helpful definition: 'Put simply, we receive his love for us and love him back in return . . . contemplation is love on fire with devotion.'[10]

We have already mentioned Augustine, who 'had in my heart infused the light of full certainty and all the gloom of doubt vanished away'; and Ignatius, who 'saw clearly . . . the holy child Jesus, at the sight of which he received the most abundant consolation'.

To these moments of vision or contemplation in history, we can add Blaise Pascal, who in 1654 saw 'from about half past ten in the evening until about half past twelve FIRE. God of Abraham, God of Isaac, God of Jacob, not of the philosophers and scholars. Certitude. Feeling. Joy. Peace.'

George Fox 'was taken up in the love of God . . . and I therein saw clearly that all was done and to be done in and by Christ . . . then I saw how he sat as a refiner's fire'. His vision was defined by 'fire'.

George Whitefield cried out after a long winter, 'I thirst,' and then it was that 'after a long night of desertation, the Star . . . the Day Star arose in my heart and . . . the spirit of God did take possession of my soul and, as I humbly hope, seal me unto the day of redemption'.

David Brainerd, also after a long dark night of the soul, found at last that

> unspeakable glory seemed to open to the view and apprehension of my soul. I do not mean any external brightness, for I saw no such thing; nor do I intend any imagination of a body of light, somewhere in the third heavens, or anything of that nature; but it was a new inward apprehension or view that I had of God, such as I never had before, nor any thing which had the least resemblance of it. I stood still; wondered; and admired! . . . My soul rejoiced with joy unspeakable, to see such a God . . . My soul was so captivated and delighted with the excellency, loveliness, greatness, and other perfections of God, that I was even swallowed up in him . . .

Charles Finney puts it like this:

> There was no fire, and no light in the room; nevertheless it appeared to me as if it were perfectly light. As I went in and shut the door after me, it seemed as if I met the Lord Jesus face to face. It did not occur to me then, nor did it for some time afterward, that was wholly a mental state. On the contrary it seemed to me that I saw him as I would see any

other man. He said nothing, but looked at me in such a manner as to break me right down at his feet. I have always since regarded this as a most remarkable state of mind; for it seemed to me a reality, that he stood before me, and I fell down at his feet and poured out my soul to him. I wept aloud like a child, and made such confessions as I could with my choked utterance. It seemed to me that I bathed his feet with my tears; and yet I had no distinct impression that I touched him, that I recollect.'

With these epiphanies in mind, it is worth asking what we can do to see this well. For Finney this seeing was 'a wholly mental state'. So I am not talking about physical eyesight, but spiritual eyes, with a special eye-salve that enables them to see. In his classic book *Prayer*, Richard Foster follows his discourse on contemplative prayer with a passage entitled 'Oregon Epiphany'. He talks of a time of strong awareness of God's presence, followed by 'seeing' God's message to him as he gazed at the beauty of his surroundings. He talks of 'seeing what had been hidden from my view'. As C.S. Lewis's Aslan, in *The Voyage of the Dawn Treader*, says: 'I have been here all the time . . . but you have just made me visible.'

The Bible retains mystery concerning this: in chapter 4 of Revelation we meet some creatures apparently especially designed for contemplation, looking on the Lord. These mysterious creatures are 'full of eyes in front and behind'. They are the four living creatures: lion, ox, man and eagle. They have eyes 'all around and within'. They are designed to behold: to contemplate. And their constant song, having seen, is to cry, 'Holy holy holy is the Lord God Almighty.'

If the creatures closest to God have multiple eyes, we want to think carefully about the necessity for seeing. The medieval monastery of St Victor in Paris had a theory that there were three ways of seeing: the first with the eyes of the flesh (thought or sight), by which we see physical reality; the second with the eyes of reason (meditation or reflection), by which we see sense. The third was with the eyes of true understanding (contemplation), by which we see spiritually.[11] Each eye raises the level of the gaze to the next, thereby overcoming one's sense of incompatibility between the physical world, reason, and the sacred.

This week, at times, I have sat in front of a bay window overlooking the sea. It is a stunning and ever-changing view of Welsh coastland and estuary. I have taken in the colours and beauty – greys and browns and blues and greens, dull tones that on careful appreciation are in fact near perfection. This has been an aesthetic treat. Secondly, and at the same time, birds of rare or common beauty have swept overhead or arrived as the tide retreated, and I have marvelled at the ornithological miracles they represent. Then, thirdly, I have 'seen' the Lord. Not with physical eyes, but in the way described above. I have meditated on Christ walking to his anxious disciples across the stormy seas. I have seen him get in the boat with a word to the raging soul and the roaring waters: 'Take courage! It is I. Don't be afraid.'[12]

Newport Epiphany

Facing the high tide and seeing salvation
Glimpsing God and heaven open
As clouds roll in from the sea
You are here
And all makes sense
I am your small sheep

I know your voice and
You know my name and
I follow you
Nothing will snatch me
From my Father's hand because
My Father is greater than all
And I am yours

O great Shepherd of my soul
Let me love you more
And those you love
All mankind
My enemies
My friends
Those who hate you
Those who love you
Lead me where you would have me go

My plea to God is to be led where he would have us go in terms of his rest and his peace and his easy yoke, that we may daily see his glory.

Collect for Contemplation

Almighty God, who did reveal yourself to Moses, to Daniel, to Stephen and to your servants the prophets: mercifully grant that we, seeking to see you in the place of prayer, might see heaven opened and Jesus at the right hand of God. Amen.

PART II: ABIDE

Whether by means of a Day Star in the East, or by means of some other transfiguration or unveiling, we have been invited to 'come and see'. We now turn to consider the challenge of 'abiding'. This is the privilege of falling in love, of intimacy, of 'kissing the Son' as Psalm 2 calls it, and of learning to stay close through times of trial, suffering and winter.

Abide in me, as I also abide in you.
(John 15:4 paraphrase)

Christ is a jewel worth more than a thousand worlds, as all know who have him. Get him, and get all; miss him and miss all . . . He is a portion that punctually, exactly and directly suits the condition of the soul, that suits the desires of the soul; the necessities of the soul, the wants of the soul, the longings of the soul, and the prayers of the soul. The soul can crave nothing, nor wish for nothing, but what is to be found in this Portion.

He is light to enlighten the soul, wisdom to counsel the soul, power to support the soul, goodness to supply the soul, mercy to pardon the soul, beauty to delight the soul, glory to ravish the soul, and fullness to fill the soul.

Thomas Brooks

. . . he is altogether lovely.

Song of Songs 5:16

CHAPTER SEVEN

Falling: The dazzling beauty of the bridegroom

As we come to consider the question of what it means to 'abide', we remember that the Bible is shot through with epiphanies, revelations, or unveilings – times when God comes near. We find them in almost every book of the Bible. Sometimes these discoveries seem to compound mysteriously with others as they take us into intimacy. In this chapter, we join the bride of Solomon's Song of Songs, who describes her beloved as 'dazzling'. Solomon was present as principal actor in the dedication of the Temple, when the heavens split open to reveal God's goodness.

It was Solomon who put into verse a love affair between a prince and a princess, in the Song of Songs. Many interpret this as being also an allegory of the love of the Church for the Son of God. Hudson Taylor's commentary on the book describes the journey of the Christian from fear and fallen-ness to discovering how to abide forever in Christ. He called it *Union and Communion*. In the Song of Songs, Solomon has his bride 'see' at last the absolutely outstanding beauty of the bridegroom: 'Outstanding among ten thousand'. Although I find it challenging, even disturbing, to try and comprehend God in this way, I want to see and understand this beauty described by Solomon. This is quite a contrast to the sheer majesty described by John on Patmos in the book of Revelation. But this contrasting nature of Christ is a fact of his character: we may need an epiphany to see it. But maybe this description, from twentieth-century Scottish preacher James Stewart, will help. He puts it thus:

He was the meekest and lowliest of all the sons of men and yet he spoke of coming on the clouds of the glory of God.

He was so austere that evil spirits and demons cried out in terror at his coming; yet he was so genial and winsome that the children liked to play with him and nestle within his arms.

His presence at a village wedding was like the presence of sunshine.

No one was half as kind and compassionate to sinners and yet no one spoke such scorching words against sin.

He was the one who washed the disciples' feet, yet strode into the temple and the moneychangers fell over themselves in their mad rush to escape the fire blazing in his eyes.

He saved others but he did not save himself.

There is nothing like the union of contrasts. The mystery of Jesus is the mystery of divine personality.

Here are the two descriptions of Christ from Revelation and the Song of Songs contrasted side by side:

His head and hair were white like wool, as white as snow, and his eyes were like blazing fire. His feet were like bronze glowing in a furnace, and his voice was like the sound of rushing waters. In his right hand he held seven stars, and out of his mouth came a

His head is purest gold; his hair is wavy and black as a raven. His eyes are like doves by the water streams, washed in milk, mounted like jewels. His cheeks are like beds of spice yielding perfume. His lips are like lilies dripping with myrrh. His arms are

sharp double-edged sword. His face was like the sun shining in all its brilliance. When I saw him, I fell at his feet as though dead. Then he placed his right hand on me and said: 'Do not be afraid.'
Revelation 1

rods of gold set with chrysolite. His body is like polished ivory decorated with sapphires. His legs are pillars of marble set on bases of pure gold. His appearance is like Lebanon, choice as its cedars. His mouth is sweetness itself; he is altogether lovely. This is my lover, this is my friend, O daughters of Jerusalem.
Song of Songs 5

One of these visions is cosmic and kingly and even fearful, whereas the other is intimate, affectionate and personal. The Church Fathers spent much time preaching and unveiling this Song of Songs text. The evangelical preacher C.H. Spurgeon said that when faced with the beauty of Christ seen in the Song, 'Love often becomes a mystic and speaks in mystic language, into which the stranger intrudes not'[1], and the Church Fathers unanimously took the passage above to be a sight of Christ's beauty. So we will join them in daring to speak of the different physical attributes of this prince, the fairest among ten thousand. All these attributes contribute to the revelation of the inner beauty of his character. The bride considers the appearance of her beloved from head to toe and gladly tells us of the dazzling, outstanding beauty of her bridegroom.

His head (leadership, or headship) is purest gold
This revelation that Christ is the head of the Church is full of consequences for our trust in his ways. 'He leads me by still

waters,' says the psalmist.[2] His head is of purest gold, 'because of the goodness of the Deity, that is, the gold of the land of the living surpasses all things that have been made by him . . . for he is so brilliant that he cannot be seen by human eyes and those who live in the flesh'.[3] John of Ford has this: 'His head is the finest gold. He is in the heart of the Father where he peers into the depths of the riches of his wisdom and knowledge. He is in the soul of the Father, where he searches out the treasures of wisdom and benevolence. He is in the holy place of God's righteousness, penetrating all the depths of his judgments and the secrets of his decrees.'[4]

For me, his head being of 'purest gold' means his leadership, which has been refined (or made perfect through suffering), can also lead us through our own painful refining. This is a great comfort to know, and can help us trust him. Some time ago I went through some painful things in the church body I was leading at that time. My saintly former college principal, Alec Motyer, got to hear about it – this is an extract from the letter he wrote to me at the time:

Your dear friends came by last Friday and let me know that you have passed through trying and stressful circumstance in the church . . . Please God the stressful times are becoming history. They may or may not be productive of evident blessing but, if the Lord should will to unroll the scroll of the eternal future, you will see that everything has not only worked for good but for very good indeed. The great thing – indeed, in ultimate terms, the only thing, is to keep our eyes turned on Jesus.

He went on to speak of the recent, unexpected death of his wife in completely trusting terms: 'She slipped off Home

bathed in the most perfect, even tangible peace. It was not
that we expected this; it leapt upon us. Heaven came to earth.
The gap left by her going is deep and wide. Life has but now
no earthly focal point, but otherwise is proving manageable
– though I would be hard put to define what manageable
means.' Here is a man who has absolute trust in the pure and
perfect headship and leadership of Christ in his life. He trusts
that 'His head is purest gold'. Few perhaps are those who
know it so implicitly.

His hair is wavy and black as a raven

Wavy hair is a prophetic echo of a group of men set apart,
like Samuel or the Nazirites of old, Samson or, later, John
the Baptist, whose dedication was expressed in not letting
a razor touch their head. These were a company of dedicated servant leaders prophetically pointing forward to
the One who was completely dedicated, sold out, given
over to the purposes of God. There was no mixture or
compromise in Christ, whose life flowed with holiness like
his flowing hair.

Some medieval commentators said that 'by saying black
like a raven she points to the hiding place of veiled mysteries . . . concealed by great darkness, as the prophet David
said: "Clouds and thick darkness are round about him."'[5]

His eyes are like doves by the water streams

His knowledge is perfect without deformity. We could spend
a week meditating on his eyes. They were clear and strong;
piercing like fire; yet limpid with love. 'Jesus looked at him
and loved him', it was said of his gaze on the departing rich
young ruler.[6] Psalm 33:18 says: '. . . the eyes of the LORD are
on those who fear him, on those whose hope is in his

unfailing love.' The bride has had an epiphany of what love looks like; she is saying: 'You haven't overlooked me. You have skilful discernment to know where I am.' It is important for us to know his omniscience. This keeps us from fear or sin. But it also encourages us through trials and tribulation. She knows his discernment of what she needs is complete and perfect.

His cheeks are like beds of spice yielding perfume
For James Durham, whose commentary was first published in 1668 and received a glowing commendation even in his own time from the great Scottish divine John Owen,[7] the sweet-smelling cheeks 'must be somewhat whereby Christ becomes sensibly sweet and refreshful to the soul's senses than flowers of perfume are for the bodily senses; therefore his love is compared to ointment.' Mike Bickle finds 'His cheeks, his emotions are like "banks of scented herbs".' He comments that there are so many different types of emotions that are fragrant, that are pleasing to us. Many people think that the only emotion God has is joy when they become Christians, alongside his anger and wrath for all wrongdoing. 'But his emotions are heaps of diverse, sweet fragrances to us. Jesus' emotional make-up is filled with passion and delight and longing for you. Jesus also has a passion for his Father, his creation, his holiness, his kingdom and so on.[8] They are tremendous and dignified yet also effervescent with the joy coming from him.'[9] It is noteworthy that the bridegroom of the Song of Songs says of the bride: 'You have stolen my heart with one glance of your eyes.'[10] It may take an epiphany, but we need to understand that although this is the Maker of the universe, you or I or the Church (at whatever level we are reading this passage) can, it seems, affect his heart with one

glance of our eyes of love and faith directed to him. This is no stoic deity without feeling but a passionate lover of our souls, thank God – may we love him back!

His lips are like lilies dripping with myrrh
His words have the sweetness of lilies. They are read more, quoted more, believed more and translated more – they are the greatest words ever spoken. Theologian Bernard Ramm has said about Jesus' words: 'Their greatness lies in the pure lucid spirituality in dealing clearly, definitively, authoritatively with the greatest problems that throb in the human breast . . . They are the kind of words and the kind of answers we would expect God to give.'[11] Yet with all their authority and power, they are lilies dripping with myrrh. Equally, his words woo me out of a life of self-indulgence, as myrrh evokes death on the cross – and the necessity of my death to self. These words concern redemption and the cross.

His arms are rods of gold set with chrysolite
His arms, symbolising his powerful actions, are royal, golden and bejewelled. This is for the works in which his strength and skill are shown. His works in redemption, when he stretches forth his arms and hands on the cross, are of infinite skill, wisely contrived and exquisitely executed.

His body is like polished ivory decorated with sapphires
Older versions (for example the KJV) translate body as 'belly' here. Even older ones translate it as 'bowels'. It is the same Hebrew word as that used in Isaiah 63:15 of the 'bowels of mercy' of God to his people. It is to be found again in Jeremiah 31:20, which says, 'my bowels are troubled for him'

(Darby Translation). James Durham explains it as referring to the bridegroom's depths of love: 'The words at first signify the intense love and tender affection wherewith our Lord Jesus (who is full of grace) is filled and "stuffed" for the good of his people; so that no mother is so compassionately affected towards the fruit of her womb as she is for her own.' He concludes that 'there is nothing that will contribute to make believers see Jesus as lovely to them as right apprehension of his love: this is the constraining, ravishing, engaging, and soul-inebriating consideration of Christ, conceiving him rightly in his admirable love "which passeth knowledge"'[12] (Ephesians 3:19). Such is the diamond-like nature of his love: it is tender but tough, like carved ivory, rare and expensive.

His legs are pillars of marble set on bases of pure gold. His appearance is like Lebanon, choice as its cedars. His mouth is sweetness itself

The way he operates his eternal plan and the way he fulfils his divine purpose are durable and stable and beautiful – just like pillars of marble. His appearance is tall, stately, honourable and fragrant (like the cedar trees of Lebanon), and there is nothing sweeter than his mouth or his kisses. This last idea is challenging and we will take the whole of the next chapter to unpack what the kiss of God means. But such is the sighting of Solomon of the beauty of Christ. It is so majestic that the bride cries out in conclusion: 'He is altogether lovely. This is my lover' adding also that he is 'my friend'. Deep calls to deep: it is intimate and immensely challenging. As we shall see, many have found this little book to be one more example of epiphany in discovering a vocabulary for loving God with all our heart, mind, soul and strength.

Collect for Falling

Lord God, your appearance indeed is altogether lovely. Your leadership and your love are altogether trustworthy. You are our beloved and you are our friend. Mercifully grant that we beholding your beauty might become beautiful like you, who are the fairest among ten thousand. Amen.

At that first kiss I felt
Something melt inside me
That hurt in an exquisite way
All my longings, all my dreams, and sweet anguish,
All the secrets that slept within me came awake,
Everything was transformed and enchanted
And made sense.
Herman Hesse, *Narcissus and Goldmund*

Let him kiss me with the kisses of his mouth –
for your love is more delightful than wine.
Song of Songs 1:2

CHAPTER EIGHT

Kissing: The intimacy of the Song of Songs

At the heart of this 'book of books', the Bible, lies the love song, the Song of Songs. Sandwiched between Ecclesiastes and Isaiah lies this jewel of a book. Between the sadness of Solomon and the comfort of the coming Christ, this song shines like a mysterious pearl in the sea. If you blink you might miss it, so short are its few pages, its 117 verses. And many do miss it, or miss its meaning. And yet it is known as 'the greatest of all the songs', 'the best of all songs', or simply 'The Song of Songs'. Why is it that through the centuries, this little poem has held some of the most effective disciples enthralled for life? Why is it that as the twenty-first century comes of age, new readers are meditating on this love song? What can it bring to the melee of worry and hurry that is our lot in life? I believe the Song is the greatest song because it looks at the subject of greatest importance. This is, it seems to me, the one thing needful, the thing that matters most in this transitory life: our love relationship, one might even say love affair – or lack of it, with the living God.

As I have said, I am writing this book for those who are coming to realise that this is *the* life and death subject. Keeping love for God burning and not letting that fire go out is the key to everything, the one thing that Christ is calling for and seeking. The Song of Songs is really about fulfilling the commandment of commandments. I believe it gives keys to finding, gaining and maintaining a capacity to love God strongly and hence to love others sweetly, despite the waves of suffering that crash over us all. The fact is, so few of us do love God today with heart, soul, mind and strength.

Many may give assent to this in their hearts, but not quite know where to go from here. The Bible offers a startling image for intimacy with God, namely the kiss: 'Let him kiss me with the kisses of his mouth – for your love is more delightful than wine.'[1] This is the celebrated start to this Song of Songs. It is intimate, personal, challenging – and even off-putting to those of a reserved temperament, like many of Anglo-Saxon or Asian background. Some make this more palatable by translating it 'the kisses of his Word', but even so, it cannot but lead us into this call to intimacy with God. Put plainly: Do I desire to be 'kissed by God'? If I do, what does this mean and how does it work?

The truth is that this tiny phrase has multiple many-layered – and ultimately nourishing – interpretations. Some Church Fathers said that it means welcoming the incarnation: the kissing of humanity and coming into flesh of God. For Origen it meant this, but also the teachings of Christ. 'For the kisses of Christ are those that he bestowed on the Church when in his advent he himself present in the flesh spoke to it words of faith and love and peace.'[2] So it means loving the Word and meditating on it, even in a biblically illiterate generation.

Kisses here indicate the birth, the teachings and also the death of Christ. During the Welsh revival the hymn 'Here Is Love Vast as the Ocean', the so-called love song of the revival, was composed and sung, with the lines:

On the mount of crucifixion,
Fountains opened deep and wide;
Through the floodgates of God's mercy
Flowed a vast and gracious tide.
Grace and love, like mighty rivers,
Poured incessant from above,
Heaven's peace and perfect justice
Kissed a guilty world in love.[3]

Here the kiss of God is lauded as the pouring out of his love upon the cross. Then for others, this 'kiss' has meant the intimacy of relationship with the Holy Spirit. Twentieth-century British evangelist David Watson used to say (drawing on Bernard de Clairvaux), 'Lovers have many ways to tell each other of their love: the word, the touch, a letter or a kiss. In the same way Christ is the Word of God, the Bible His love letter, but the Spirit is His kiss . . .' He would preach that his listeners seek to be 'kissed by God', to receive the fullness of the Holy Spirit. Incidentally, it may be that a reluctance to embrace the manifest experience of this sealing – or to put it more poetically, the 'kissing' – of the Holy Spirit is responsible for the reluctance of some to dare to read the Song of Songs allegorically.

Others, in this verse, see the soul of the Christian saying, 'Let him kiss me'. Scottish preacher James Durham builds on this, suggesting, 'By "kisses," we understand most lovely, friendly, familiar and sensible manifestations of his love . . . Let him, who is the most excellent and singular person in the world, kiss me, a contemptible, despicable creature.'[4]

Another commentator, James Pennington, continues: 'What is the kiss of your mouth? It is where the human and divine become completely one. How much we struggle with the belief that you divine lover really love this poor little human so plagued with sin and infidelity: O give me the kisses of your mouth!'[5] Back in medieval times, Bernard de Clairvaux (author of the hymn 'O Sacred Head Sore Wounded') felt this has to do with refreshment for the one who is fulfilling the commandments, trying to obey the devout life, but utterly dry: 'True it may be I am fulfilling the commandments in one way or another, but "my soul is like earth without water" (Psalm 142:6). Therefore if my whole burnt offering is to become worthy, Let him I pray and beseech "kiss me with the kisses of his mouth".'[6]

I think this is challenging for many Christians, bordering as it does on mysticism. C.H. Spurgeon came across similar reticence in his day. In his sermon on Songs 1:7, 'Love to Jesus', he says:

'Let Him kiss me with the kisses of His lips, for His love is better than wine.' 'No,' you say, 'that is too familiar for me.' Then I fear you do not love Him, for love is always familiar. Faith may stand at a distance, for her look is saving. But love comes near, for she must kiss, she must embrace. Why, Beloved, sometimes the Christian so loves his Lord that his language becomes unmeaning to the ears of others who have never been in his state. Love has a celestial tongue of her own and I have sometimes heard her speak so that men have said, 'That man rants and raves – he knows not what he says.' Hence it is that love often becomes a Mystic and speaks in mystic language, into which the stranger intrudes not.[7]

Against the charge that such 'spiritual affections' are self-indulgent and impractical, Spurgeon goes on to say:

Oh, you should see love when she has her heart full of her Saviour's presence, when she comes out of her chamber! Indeed she is like a giant refreshed with new wine. I have seen her dash down difficulties, tread upon hot irons of affliction and her feet have not been scorched. I have seen her lift up her spear against ten thousand and she has slain them at one time. I have known her give up all she had, even to the stripping of herself, for Christ, and yet she seemed to grow richer and to be decked with ornaments as she made herself poor, that she might cast her all upon her Lord and give up all to Him.

In fact, some of the most effective missionaries, taking the gospel into new cultures, have been nourished by the Song of Songs and this idea of the kiss of God. This remains a great missions need today. How does the Church address a world that does not speak her language? The nineteenth-century missioner J. Hudson Taylor was a man of such stature, in my opinion – theologically, missiologically and practically, in terms of this 'translation' between cultures – that we have not seen his like since. He was a man of extreme courage and selflessness in the face of danger. If there is revival in China today it is certainly in part due to him. During his ministry he was to be found writing on the one hand a magazine entitled simply *China's Millions*, and on the other an allegorical commentary on the Song of Songs, *Union and Communion*.[8] This is about the possibility of growing into unbroken communion with God as Hudson Taylor saw evidenced in the bride's experience in the Song of Songs.

Continuing the meditation we are engaged on: the kiss of God has been likened to a human kiss that resolves everything. Herman Hesse, in his novel *Narcissus and Goldmund*, describes it hauntingly:

At that first kiss I felt
Something melt inside me
That hurt in an exquisite way
All my longings, all my dreams, and sweet anguish,
All the secrets that slept within me came awake,
Everything was transformed and enchanted
And made sense.[9]

'Let him kiss me with the kisses of his mouth' takes on richer meaning when we realise that *proskuneo* is the most common Greek word for worship used in the New Testament. It means 'to come towards to kiss'. So this first verse of the Song of Songs describes the essence of what can be found on the lips of worshippers across the world. Psalm 2 hints at this with its mysterious last verse, 'Kiss the Son . . .'

We know that in times of revival the Song, and especially this part of the Song, seems to have become clear. We might even say that without what we might call 'revival in the heart', we will find it hard to grasp and appropriate full intimacy with God. The nineteenth-century evangelist Charles Finney used to say: 'In times of Revival the language of the Song of Songs became as natural as breathing.'[10] Jonathan Edwards, the saintly principal of Yale, spoke in like terms during the Great Awakening in the eighteenth century. His wife Sarah wrote of a personal encounter with the Holy Spirit as 'continuing all night long with a constant, clear, and lively sense of the heavenly sweetness of Christ's excellent love, of his nearness and dearness to me, and my dearness to him'.[11]

Sixteenth-century Puritan Richard Sibbes spoke of the Spirit as 'the sweet kiss of the soul' – experiencing 'spiritual ravishings, the beginning of heaven – heaven before its time'.[12] Puritan Samuel Rutherford, writing from a Scottish covenanter's jail, could write of 'a springtide of God's love'. He writes: 'My sweet Lord has taken off his mask and said "kiss thy fill" – the bridegroom's love hath run away with my heart – Oh love, love, love.'[13]

The kiss is a universal symbol of intimacy, whether between friends or lovers. The kiss of God therefore indicates a supreme experience of the presence and the love of God. As Origen said, we can indeed experience it through reading the Word of God in a quiet time of meditation, alone with God or in a crowd. I would say the 'kisses of his Word' are to be experienced daily. But just as in a marriage we need to take time to kiss, and it may take the right atmosphere and a certain 'settling down' into affectionate communication, in the same way we may feel we cannot rush into the kisses of God, but that they are to be cultivated, and asked for, as a bride may ask her husband or a husband his bride. Someone said: 'Is not the kiss the very autograph of love?'[14] We kiss him; but also, he kisses us. When a newlywed husband is told: 'You may now kiss the bride', whoever heard of a bride who replied: 'No, I don't like kissing.' It may be challenging, in that it is intimate and to proceed we have to drop our guard and remove our masks. But it is not to be missed.

This in turn brings transformation. In children's fables, a kiss awakened Sleeping Beauty; a kiss turned the frog into a prince. 'Soul meets soul on lovers' lips,'[15] said Shelley, and another said: 'When I kiss you, I can taste your soul.'[16] So it is that the kiss of God implies 'connection'. Remembering our thoughts on the transfiguration, we might say it is a mountain-top experience. And on a mountain-top we may feel especially 'connected' to the Creator. It is interesting that Psalm 19, as well as speaking of the heavens telling of the glory of God and pouring out speech, also describes the sun coming out as 'like a bridegroom'. So when we feel 'connected', we may say that the kiss of God is an appropriate way to describe it. Furthermore, Psalm 85:10–11 suggests a kissing of heaven and humankind when justice is on the earth. Often those involved in such work are themselves very connected people: 'Love and faithfulness meet together; righteousness and peace kiss each other. Faithfulness springs forth from the earth, and righteousness looks down from heaven.'

The Song of Songs adds more to our understanding if we read on from those first lines: 'Let him kiss me with the kisses of his mouth – for your love is more delightful than wine. Pleasing is the fragrance of your perfumes; your name is like perfume poured out.'[17]

Even the best wine, if you have too much of it, will leave you with a hangover. The kiss of God is better than wine! Wine may be given up for it – sometimes fasting from wine and food will help us to enter into a season of encounter with God, and to experience the kisses of God.

This discipline, of course, has an ancient pedigree. Of the young John the Baptist, it was promised, 'He is never to take wine',[18] echoing the call of that rare group of people in the Old Testament, the Nazirites, who so wanted God and his kingdom that they lived lifestyles that were set apart for God, lives that included seasons of fasting to show their devotion to God. Daniel and his friends were a similar company, who refused a hostile society's fine foods and wines. In an alien culture, they heard God and changed history. And today, I know of young, set-apart leaders who will declare a year's fast from alcohol in order to draw near to God, because they know that his love is better than wine and they long to focus on it. Always, in my observation, the results are powerful.

The kiss leads to awareness of the smell of the other – the scent of holiness. 'Your name is like perfume poured out.' The 'fragrance of your perfumes' suggests the aroma of Christ, and looks forward to Paul's insight to the Corinthians: 'But thanks be to God, who . . . through us spreads everywhere the fragrance of the knowledge of him. For we are to God the aroma of Christ . . .'[19]

The perfumed ointment can mean the virtues of the Holy Spirit, fragrance coming from the character of the Holy Spirit smelt on believers. The name of Jesus is also powerful. Some have felt it is like music from a far country. And to rehearse the names of Christ is like healing ointment. There is an old song: 'Thy name is as ointment poured forth: Jesus.'[20] This echoes Gregory the Great, who wrote: 'Your name is an unguent poured out of its divine immensity for the sake of our nature; from being invisible it renders itself visible . . .' He then remembers Christ 'emptied himself taking the form of a servant' and says: 'What Paul calls "emptied" Solomon calls "emptied out".' Since then the Lord has been made known to the human race by the humility of the incarnation; it is said to him: 'Your name is like ointment poured out.'[21]

We come back, pleasingly, to the idea mentioned above of 'fragrant saints'. Those who are kissed by the kindness and presence of Christ will find his fragrance imparted to them: they will themselves become fragrant.

Later we read: 'My lover is to me a sachet of myrrh, resting . . .' (Songs 1:13). Somehow, mysteriously, the aroma of Christ comes to perfume the bride of Christ. In this particular case the perfume is identified as myrrh: the aroma associated with suffering and preservation in the face of death. One Church Father, Nilus of Ancyra, movingly comments: 'She calls Him "sachet of myrrh" on account of his suffering and his death and the apparent disgrace that derives from the cross when he compressed the power of the Godhead, inactive, into his body as into a tiny bag.'[22]

Let me end this meditation on the 'kisses of God' with the following reflection. Such intimate experiences serve to draw us further and deeper into our walk with God and our love for Christ. They draw us into this privileged position of 'abiding', of resting, of remaining – of continuing in the love of God and living in his embrace.

In chapter 2:6–7 we find: 'His left arm is under my head, and his right arm embraces me. Daughters of Jerusalem, I charge you by the gazelles and by the does of the field: Do not arouse or awaken love until it so desires.'

Three times in the Song of Songs comes the mysterious phrase 'do not awaken love until it so desires'.[23] This can be read as an instruction to 'abide' and not to just hurry on to the next thing. Rather the presence of God (his arm protecting us) is so pleasant as to be treasured and enjoyed for as long as possible. Thus Durham again: 'If a sensible presence be not tenderly entertained, it will not last. Believers should be most careful then when they are admitted to near and sensible fellowship with Christ, that nothing may fall out which may provoke him to depart . . . The least sinful motions should be suppressed as having a great tendency to stir up the beloved to be gone.'[24]

If these testimonies intrigue and inspire you, then take time to ask God for such a revelation for yourself. Speak to him clearly and, in the quiet place of personal prayer, make the experience of this revelation your request and prayer pilgrimage from now on. You will surely not be disappointed.

Collect for Kissing

Lord Jesus, you taught us at all times and in all places to be ready for you: our coming bridegroom. Mercifully grant that we may receive that grace of which your prophet speaks, and kiss us with the kisses of your Word. May our souls be warmed by your ever-fragrant love, that we may carry the aroma of that same love into our homes and into our land. We ask this by your merits alone. Amen.

I have gone backward in the work,
The labour has not sped,
Drowsy and dark my spirit lies,
Heavy and dull as lead.
How can I rouse my sinking soul
From such a lethargy?
How can I break these iron chains,
And set my spirit free?
My sins increase, my love grows cold,
And Hope within me dies,
And Faith itself is wavering now,
O how shall I arise!
Anne Brontë, 'Despondency'

Love is enough: though the World be a-waning,
And the woods have no voice but the voice of complaining,
Though the sky be too dark for dim eyes to discover
The gold-cups and daisies fair blooming thereunder,
Though the hills be held shadows, and the sea a dark wonder,
And this day draw a veil over all deeds pass'd over,
Yet their hands shall not tremble, their feet shall not falter;
The void shall not weary, the fear shall not alter
These lips and these eyes of the loved and the lover.
William Morris, 'Love Is Enough'

Many waters cannot quench love . . .
Song of Songs 8:7

CHAPTER NINE

Surviving

One of Jesus' tougher sayings has to do with love. Looking into the future of human civilisation, he warns: 'Because of the increase of wickedness, the love of most will grow cold.'[1] This chapter addresses the issue of maintaining and sustaining love even in the driest desert and coldest winter.

Despite difficult circumstances, on every continent there are banners of love being unfurled and rivers of compassion flowing to the poorest of the poor. But there is also intense trouble and battle. Things happen in life, so many things, to quench – or at least weaken – love. It may not be wickedness attacking, but sheer hard work, the dance of juggling so many responsibilities with career, family, relationships. Or disappointment and failure may come, to say nothing of tragedy, which comes crashing over us. What should be a dance becomes drudgery.

For in any life there will be winter, there will be night or deep darkness, there will be desert and there will be flood waters. They may come as a result of bereavement, depression, sickness, or a breakdown in relationships. Or there may be circumstances of debt or disaster; or simply, in the midst of apparent normality, the absence of God or gladness.

Perhaps the greatest skill to learn in life is how to travel through such troubled times, how to survive them as we proceed on our journey.

How do we get warm when the love of God feels freezing cold and we fear we might die of exposure in discontented winter?

How do we see when we are in the middle of the darkest of all dark nights and the blackness of the absence of hope is almost crushing us to death?

What direction can we find when all we can see is wilderness and drear desert?

Who will throw us a lifeline when we feel we are drowning, choking for air in the flood waters?

These four – cold winter of death or bereavement; dark night of doubt or atheism; parched desert of depression or despair; and overwhelming waters of disaster, like a tsunami – take us into terrain that is tough indeed, but familiar to many more people than we might imagine. Yet in this age of the pursuit of pleasure few are the voices that will help us. I hope here to point to places of warmth in the winter, streams in the desert, light in the night, and shelter from the waterstorm that can flood over us.

I am writing for those who know about these things. I am writing for those in the middle of them. I am writing for those in the Arctic winter, the unending darkness, bone-dry badlands; for those in life-threatening storms – and, too, for those wanting to walk with others through them. There is a range of rugged landscape or threatening climate in life. And the doors through which we enter will be these four key images of winter, night, desert and waters.

These four landscapes or climates are all found in the love poem attributed to Solomon that we have been dwelling on previously. Good poetry crushes the dirty coals of truth into diamonds. Perhaps that compression of truth into its essence is the reason I have found the Song of Songs so eloquent, even epiphanic concerning suffering. Some have found its words perplexing and some have limited it to a treatise on sex, or passionate monogamy – which is what it certainly is. But many of our most effective leaders have found it to be an inspiration for all of life. Spurgeon (prince of nineteenth-century preachers) said that 'although we see our Saviour's face on every page of the Bible, it is here (in the Song) that we hear his heart and feel his love for us'.[2] Spurgeon was one who through long seasons of depression knew what it was to need comfort in the dark night.

We begin with winter. Nearly thirty years ago, our first son died unexpectedly, suddenly, in his cot. It was 'cot death' – Sudden Infant Death Syndrome (SIDS). We were working in the USA at the time, had been out at a meeting, and returned home only to be rushed to the hospital where our beloved Samuel had been taken. I remember our rising panic in the car and then being taken into a room with a TV mumbling aimlessly in the background and hearing the horror of the words from the doctor: 'The child is not alive.' Then holding the little scrap, already cold in my arms, and praying for God to raise him from the dead, but to no avail. I remember staying, praying on and weeping on, but then in the end, all too soon, having to leave him there – alone, never to see him again on this earth, this small person we had only known for nine short weeks. I remember returning to our two little daughters and explaining as best we could to a two and a four year old what had happened. Even now, as I write, I grieve and mourn. I remember the dark days beginning and going on greyly, seemingly forever, without any colour in them. I remember our daughter coming into our bedroom early one morning and asking us: 'Did we take some of Samuel's clothes for him into heaven because otherwise he might be cold there?' Why is it that still today that question undoes me?

Even as I write the words, the memories of that bleak midwinter day come rushing back to me. In the popular novel *The Shack* the death of a child is referred to as the 'Great Sadness'[3]. I used to think such an event and its 'Great Sadness' pretty rare. But I have come to realise that most people, if not all, walk through a winter of bereavement – to do with the death of a person or the death of a dream – for stretches of life. We may feel such times should be an exception and are to be snapped out of. Christians particularly may feel that they should be the happiest people on earth and that, if they don't have an upbeat attitude and optimistic faith, then they are a failure at life. But to try to have such a positive attitude when the world seems cold feels wrong and is not true either to oneself or to the circumstances.

On that bleak day, our world lost all its colour at a stroke, turning to sunless grey. I remember hunching my shoulders and bracing myself at death's icy blast. I pushed the friend I was with to pray and I prayed too for resurrection from the dead, for springtime after the winter. But no answer came; not of the kind I wanted. And so a cold and constrained time began for me, and did not end for three years. This is the experience of winter. We might think winter should only last three months before spring comes. But there can be parts of our lives, and there are parts of the world, where it never ends. In Lewis's Narnia, the effect of the white witch's occupation is that it is 'always winter but never Christmas'. The Song of Songs is eloquent often in what it leaves unsaid and this is true of its description of how the winter ends. The Song simply says that it is over. In one of the best-loved verses of the Bible, often quoted at weddings, the beloved 'darling' Church is told: 'Arise, my darling, my beautiful one, and come with me. See! The winter is past; the rains are over and gone. Flowers appear on the earth; the season of singing has come . . .'[4]

Before this, however, who knows how long has been the winter?

My own experience of coping with bereavement following the loss of our child was that it took time. Time is a healer, I believe, but so much time! One thing to do if you are in that winter is to seek warmth by the fire of his love: simply to lean on God for patience and keep warm close to him. His word is a warming comfort. Psalms expressing forsakenness but ending with hope in God – of which there are, thankfully, so many (among Psalms 30–90 for example) – and psalms of ascents (such as 120–130) were invaluable. At the worst times I found they were just enough each day to stop frost-bite setting in. Then, at a certain time on a certain day, the sun came out and it seemed that, for me, the winter was over. It was almost exactly three years after the event itself. I was in a church leaders' meeting in Essex. I remember the place – a pew – and the moment: during the coffee break. A preacher prayed for me and said, 'Come, Holy Spirit.' I waited on God and slowly but surely the sunshine broke in. I felt hope. As if to accompany this, I felt as though a heavy weight were on me – like the weight of glory. Pretty soon I had to sit down under this. I was surrounded by Love. I felt I heard God saying that I was his son, his beloved. I could not under-stand why my son had died. These things happen. But all would be well. Indeed, I realised with a flash of relief that all was very well. I emerged from the epiphany humbled, trans-formed, hopeful. I don't know why this happened when it did. Maybe it was just that the time had come.

Others will find there is a less instantaneous exit. They will live through a change in the seasons that comes more slowly and uncertainly, with unexpected reversals to winter. Getting out of your winter may take time. It seems never-ending and this does not suit our culture, which is accustomed to the supply of instant heat. Halogen brightness removes any chill in an instant, and many would-be encouragers will encourage the bereaved to 'move on'. These 'time-to-move-on' people are like Job's comforters, however. For the winter takes time to pass. I write in a Europe where the climate is changing: it can still be snowing in the South of France in April. But I know that 'this too will pass'.

What of the night?

I quite often sit listening alongside people who are in the night. They grope around in the dark looking for a sense of the presence of God, which once they knew but now feel they have lost. It is as if the light they need to show the way is simply gone. I think of the brilliant teacher we know who winsomely tells her children about the love of God while at the same time secretly questioning whether he exists at all because of the suffering she sees in the world. I think of the film producer I know who just cannot break through into the presence of God and has put his faith on hold as he walks through the darkness. This is the dark night of the soul.

There is a demonic dimension to this darkness when the voice of anti-Christ is calling so stridently to our nation, 'There is no God.' I believe that my country, Britain, is in the middle of a season of darkness. Whether advertised on buses or broadcast on TV chat shows, the darlings of our culture are, by and large, godless. My own city, Oxford, is the seat of a phenomenon called the 'New Atheism', which masquerades as scientific but is in fact merely soulless and strident in its attacks against Christianity in all its forms. This is the only thing new about the new atheism: whereas before people could live in mutual respect of opinions held, it seems now that faith in God is to be hounded out of the public square. So in Britain we see a nurse suspended for praying for a patient, a marriage counsellor dismissed for his Christian conviction, a teacher suspended for questioning the new anti-Christian status quo.

Darkness is not just the result of politics, of course; it is personal, and plunges real people into a private dark night of the soul. The context of Christ's remarks about love growing cold speaks about this, saying: 'You will be hated by all nations because of me. At that time many will turn away from the faith and will betray and hate each other, and many false prophets will appear and deceive many people. Because of the increase of wickedness, the love of most will grow cold.'[5] If you are walking through the darkness of doubt, the very atmosphere that pervades our land may be contributing to stifle and throttle your faith too.

What can come to help us in this context? Where can we find help to lighten our darkness? I believe one great source of comfort is the ancient idea of the 'Dark night of the Soul'. This Christian understanding was developed principally by John of the Cross, a sixteenth-century Spanish monk, and friend of St Teresa of Avila. The idea he developed is that God will allow the Christian to travel through darkness. It is precisely in the darkness that we will learn to lean on God. This is an invaluable lesson that with regret we must recognise can only be learnt in the darkness of suffering. So it is, paradoxically, that those who are wise will even welcome darkness. Hence John of the Cross's poem:

One dark night,
fired with love's urgent longings – ah, the sheer grace! –
I went out unseen,
my house being now all stilled.

. . .

On that glad night,
in secret, for no one saw me,
nor did I look at anything,
with no other light or guide
than the one that burned in my heart.

. . .

O guiding night!
O night more lovely than the dawn!
O night that has united
the lover with his beloved

. . .

I abandoned and forgot myself,
laying my face on my Beloved;
all things ceased; I went out from myself,
leaving my cares
forgotten among the lilies.[6]

This is great strong evocative language. The poet calls it a
'glad night'; he finds night 'more lovely than the dawn'. He
calls it a guiding night that will get his heart burning with
love for the lover of his soul. John of the Cross is drawing on
the episodes in the Song of Songs where the bride is sent out
into the night. This is her experience:

All night long on my bed I looked for the one my heart loves;
I looked for him but did not find him.
I will get up now and go about the city, through its streets

and squares; I will search for the one my heart loves. So I looked for him but did not find him.

The watchmen found me as they made their rounds in the city. 'Have you seen the one my heart loves?'

Scarcely had I passed them when I found the one my heart loves. I held him and would not let him go . . .[7]

She finds her beloved and clings to him and will not let him go. So, for us, night is helpful in (eventually) increasing the power of loving connection. But later (in chapter 5), she is again drawn out into the night and cannot find him. On this second occasion she tells how: 'The watchmen found me as they made their rounds in the city. They beat me, they bruised me; they took away my cloak, those watchmen of the walls!'[8]

Those going through the darkness today may well feel beaten up. Political leaders, probably all leaders in fact, and particularly church leaders, feel the force of this at times. They may feel the absence of God and the presence of oppressors. Church leaders may talk about 'sheep bite' as shorthand for inhouse criticism, which in times of division can turn nasty. To the ancient phrase 'wagging of tongues' can be added the new phenomenon today of 'blog snarl'. Some leaders, particularly in the political arena, are confronted with online blogging against them which can be particularly vicious because anonymous and unverifiable. Accusations are made; they may be refuted, but the urban myths established thereby will never die. In the Christian arena this happens increasingly as the fashion for 'transparency and freedom of expression' seems to trump any biblical teaching on discretion and the need for face-to-face communication. This can be part of one's darkness. But it was ever thus. 'Woe to you when all men speak well of you'[9] is one word of paradoxical comfort from Christ to hang on to in such times.

In lands under persecution, the attacks that bring on the darkness could involve imprisonment, loss of work, separation from children, even the possibility of execution. Others have walked this way before. Many of David's psalms testify to this sense of oppression, betrayal and battle. Godly lovers of the poor speak of it too. Mother Teresa of Calcutta, according to letters released in 2007, may prove the most long-term case on record of travelling through the dark night of the soul, as she tells of her struggles lasting from her first intimate deep call from God to found the Sisters of Charity in 1948, almost up until her death in 1997, with only brief interludes of relief between. Franciscan Father Benedict Groeschel, a friend of Mother Teresa for a large part of her life, claims that this inexplicable depression-like darkness left only towards the end of her life.

These times are important because they are times when we have to realise that God wants us to trust him, to hold his hand in the darkness. It will help if we understand that while we may have a simple plan for our life (to be happy, prosperous, successful and at peace), God wants us to learn to trust him deeply and against the odds. Trouble comes for us when these two programmes are going in opposite directions, for God is stronger and he will prevail. We do well when, like the bride in the Song, we learn a deeper dependence; when we decide not to be offended with God, not to accuse him of not knowing what he is doing, not to kick against his path for us, but to trust him. This is vital and will prove transformational. We become people who 'lean not on our own understanding'. We learn an eternal lesson. We can walk in his love – and give it away, whatever the metaphorical time of day! Thus, the bride in the Song, having been beaten up, when asked to tell of her beloved, says without hesitation: 'My lover is . . . outstanding among ten thousand.'[10] She utters the beautiful description of Christ that we have already dwelt on. That epiphany comes after this darkness. There is now no hint of mistrust. She has broken through to maturity. And so may we, if we will persist in treading this road less travelled.

We have considered winter and night, but the terrain we are travelling through as we seek to live a life of love may have other difficulties still to be faced: desert and waters. The danger of desert lands is evident. Without water we will die in the desert, and maybe before that we will go mad. Jesus heard voices in the wilderness telling him to throw himself off a cliff. In the wilderness, people can hear voices of suicide or self-harm. I think of the students I have known, unable to break free from the hammering compulsion to starve themselves. It doesn't seem to help to theorise that this is a way to gain control in a world that is out of control. Anorexia refuses to be rationalised away.

Depression also happens to people trying to love. Sometimes it is a result of burnout; sometimes there are other factors, chemical or emotional. I have known mothers who feel so black they want to kill themselves, fathers who cannot shake off irrational, mesmerising, death-whispering despair.

This is a 'now' subject. As I write, today's newspapers happen to contain entire supplements given over to stress. It has become almost fashionable to admit to depression, although the stories of constant panic are sometimes so harrowing that this is clearly a perverse juxtaposition. One famous depressive advises when things get black or dangerous: 'I find a quiet corner and tell myself I have known these feelings before and they pass. Sleep, sport, music, family life . . . the insight that none of us is ever truly alone, the knowledge that others feel the same things at different times in different ways . . .'[11]

I believe it is truly helpful to know that we are not alone. Others have walked these paths before and have turned them eventually into deliverance. But even more, God may be leading us into and during these desert times. He is there in them. He knows about them. And in them, he asks us to learn to lean.

The desert speaks to me also of a depressing cultural wasteland and the dust of death. I live in a city-centre environment where each weekend I see teenage or student party-night tragedies – half dressed and legless – stumbling about in the city. Western society binge-drinking itself to oblivion is like trying to drink yourself out of the desert that you have found yourself in – but the alcohol does nothing to quench the existential thirst. It only makes it worse.

If you are surrounded by – or even immersed in – this yourself, it is important to be in community, and to be able to tell the truth to others about your struggle. Hopefully this can give some solidarity, which will help you also to keep on leaning on God while madness goes on around you – for madness it is. The fact is that it is possible to keep clean and to lean on God. As we get a sight of him even in the desert, we realise anew that he is altogether lovely and waiting to reach out his hand to strengthen. And once you have learnt to do that, help others to lean on him too. Walk in love and give love away.

In speaking of the desert, that place of suffering, the Song of Songs tells of the one who in the end comes up from out of the desert, leaning on her beloved. This is a powerful image I have meditated on for years.

'Who is this coming up from the desert like a column of

smoke, perfumed with myrrh and incense made from all the spices of the merchant?'[12] asks the Song. These images speak of a person, a family, a church that has been through the myrrh of suffering, and has got the incense – the aroma of Christ – on her clothing. Again we come back to the idea of 'fragrant saints'. The Church Fathers read these evocative texts to refer to a people not afraid even to martyrdom, and some would say that a restoration of the courage of the martyrs is the great gift to pray for.

If we mature in the desert, we can learn things we would only learn there and then 'come out leaning'. I believe that, just as John the Baptist emerged out of the desert of obscurity to prepare the way for the coming of Christ, so today a generation is emerging from the wilderness, content to be faceless in hidden obedience to prepare for his second coming. When this happens it will bring a unique message for those going through the suffering washing over the world. Currently the Church has little to say to society because she is pretty unprepared to survive the desert. An unprepared Church cannot possibly prepare an unprepared world. She will be prepared by learning to love God through the desert – she will be prepared through seeing the beauty of the Lord even in the desert, and then coming out, leaning only on him.

Commenting on and broadening this interpretation, Ambrose of Milan says:

> Seeing the bride cleaving to Christ and still ascending with him – for he stoops to meet and assist those who seek him repeatedly, that he may lift them up – the daughters of Jerusalem say, 'Who is this coming up from the wilderness leaning?' This earthly place of ours appears to be an uncultivated wilderness filled with brambles and thorns of our sins,

they plainly wonder how a soul may cleave to God's word and ascend like smoke . . . that seeks the heights and then radiates a delightful fragrance'.[13]

And so it is that the aroma of Christ is around those 'suffering saints' who 'come up leaning'.

Finally, let us speak of the waters: the storms of life that threaten to overwhelm and sweep us away. On that black stormy day when, at the age of fourteen, my mother told me quietly that my father had left home for another and there would be a tragic divorce, I choked for air and tried to breathe as the waters seemed to drown me. I guess the consequences have continued all my life since. Few people escape having to live through a time in their life when circumstances are cruel and crash over them like a hurricane-fuelled flood on an unsuspecting city. Some in the twenty-first century experience this literally as natural disasters and extreme weather shake up the planet. In 2011, there were enormous floods on three different continents and Japan suffered a tsunami to rival that which a few years earlier broke over Indonesia. The awful consequences of that flood are still to be quantified as nuclear reactors have leaked radiation and potentially contaminated a whole region. Remembering Jesus' prediction – 'nations will be in anguish and perplexity at the roaring and tossing of the sea. Men will faint from terror, apprehensive of what is coming on the world' seldom has this been so relevant. Seldom also have we so needed to heed the advice which follows: 'When these things begin to take place, stand up and lift up your heads, because your redemption is drawing near.'[14]

What can the waters be? I suggest they are anything that threatens to overwhelm, to drown you. It may be tragic divorce or relationship breakdown. I have known these to cause panic attacks and near asphyxiation. People gasp for breath in the night as sleep eludes them. It may be economic recession, the flood tide of which is hitting the world like some repeat of the 1920s. It may be accident, which suddenly strikes like a flash-flood, leaving in its wake broken lives and families altered forever.

Paradoxically, it is important to add that the flood waters may on the other hand be affluence and wealth, which are like a flood of apparent goodness that is capable of choking the life out of you in the end: we need to be aware of this and to learn to give wealth away if we have it, so that we put into practice the realisation that the important thing is to lean on God, or, to put it another way, to hold on to him.

Of the waters, the Song of Songs hopefully declares: '. . . love is as strong as death . . . It burns like blazing fire, like a mighty flame. Many waters cannot quench love; rivers cannot wash it away.'[15] If we get hold of the flame of epiphany love, it is an uncontested fact that it will keep on burning right through the overflowing floods. And this is indeed what happens in times of persecution, as we shall see. The fire does not go out. The candle is lit and keeps on burning and will never go out.

The Bible does not deny that there will be flood waters. In the midst of these four scenarios of suffering – winter, night, desert and waters – through all these, our task is navigating them. We need to learn that great wisdom consists in knowing how to keep the fire burning in spite of them. It is a skill which often seems unlearnable until we are in the midst of it. A bit like learning to swim, it is impossible to start until you are in the water. The important thing, however, is not to drown in the attempt. Hopefully a father, a mother, or a friend or teacher will help us. But sometimes these are not there for us. And yet as we draw near, like Moses or like John on Patmos or Daniel or Ezekiel drawing near to the one who is a river of fire, for whom somehow the fiery love of God got inside their hearts and took them through the worst, so for us God will get us through. Ask God now for that same fire to fill your heart too and burn there, inextinguishable.

Collect for Surviving

O God, in your Son you suffered in the desert, darkness, winter and the deep waters of death. Mercifully grant that your love so burn in our heart and on our arm that we ourselves may not only survive but even thrive and in turn bring your burning love to others in darkness; through Jesus Christ our Lord. Amen.

He shewed me a little thing, the quantity of an hazel-nut, in the palm of my hand; and it was as round as a ball. I looked thereupon with eye of my understanding, and thought: What may this be? And it was answered generally thus: It is all that is made. I marvelled how it might last, for methought it might suddenly have fallen to naught for little. And I was answered in my understanding: It lasteth, and ever shall for that God loveth it. And so All-thing hath the Being by the love of God.

In this Little Thing I saw three properties. The first is that God made it, the second is that God loveth it, the third, that God keepeth it. But what is to me verily the Maker, the Keeper, and the lover, – I cannot tell; for till I am Substantially oned to Him, I may never have full rest nor very bliss: that is to say, till I be so fastened to Him, that there is right nought that is made betwixt my God and me.

The Writings of Julian of Norwich

Come to me, all you who are weary and burdened, and I will give you rest. Take my yoke upon you and learn from me, for I am gentle and humble in heart, and you will find rest for your souls. For my yoke is easy and my burden is light.

Matthew 11:28–30

CHAPTER TEN

Soul-Resting: The infinite value of the easy yoke of Christ

In all the epiphanies we have been exploring, we will guess that if it is authentic epiphany, it will lead to rest for our souls – so needed today in our world which seems to be careering out of control, not least through the ever-increasing speed of communications. Jesus expresses it definitively with his call: 'Take my yoke upon you and learn from me, for I am gentle and humble in heart, and you will find rest for your souls.' He suggests this rest is something revealed to children and not to the 'wise' – 'I thank you, Father, that you have hidden these things from the wise and understanding and revealed them to children.' The leader of today, of whatever age or situation, needs to learn childlike, counter-intuitive capacity to rest in revelation and contemplation, as I have called it. As we see the love of God poured out to us, we are set free from the striving driven-ness that plagues so many, into real rest for our souls. We now move on to list some of the consequences of this epiphany living and how it works in practice.

First, and perhaps most telling, being a lover reduces burnout. We read in the Psalms: 'He who dwells in the shelter of the Most High will rest in the shadow of the Almighty.'[1] And yet, so many today will not or cannot rest. The result is carnage: troubled marriages and poor health, absentee fathers, workaholics heading to breakdown. What is needed is a generation of centred lovers who will work from their certainty of being loved rather than to earn that love. Many Christians who reach out to others then burn out quickly because they launch into ministry before they establish the foundations of being lovers of God. Discouragement, despair, boredom and frustration will occur if we don't realise we are called to be lovers first. Yes, of course God has called us to work for his cause. Yes, we are called to bear the inconvenience of being caregivers to other people. But we must remember that such works of service are part of the second commandment; they are an overflow of the first commandment.

Some years ago a movement called 'the Toronto Blessing' – though I prefer to follow John Arnott and refer to it as 'the Father's Blessing' – broke upon an unsuspecting world Church. There were various mystical accompaniments to the movement, but one frequent experience was that people, overcome with the 'weight of glory', would literally be reduced to lying on the ground unable to move, or 'resting in the Spirit'. Exhausted, burnt-out pastors, parents and business people alike would get arrested in rest for an evening. Often what happened in these encounters seems to have been a revelation of divine Love. This revelation is well documented and matches that of English fourteenth-century mystic Julian of Norwich or Sarah (wife of Jonathan) Edwards in the eighteenth-century revival. Sadly so many experiencing this pause and rest then went straight back to a life of burnout, rather than learning the vital lesson to love and become a lover of God. Carol Arnott put it like this: 'There must be time for him, just to love him and have him love us, no other agendas, no lists of prayer requests. These may come later, but we need to put loving him first, because only as we are filled with his love do we have love to give away. So many Christians cannot rest in his presence but must constantly be on duty. I do not want to hear the words "Depart from me I never knew you". I want the love affair to grow.'[2]

Second, those who have this epiphany will find that temptation is reduced: 'I will say of the LORD, "He is my refuge and my fortress, my God, in whom I trust." Surely he will save you from the fowler's snare and from the deadly pestilence.'[3]

I believe that we are built for fascination with God. If we are not fascinated by God, we will inevitably fill the gap with other fascinations. Tozer put it thus: 'We are called to an everlasting preoccupation with God.' Our original design in the garden of Eden would suggest that we are made in God's likeness to relate to him. If we abandon this first love, we will find ourselves separated into restless addictions or temptations. One key to a great marriage and to being a great lover is to remain fascinated by your spouse. Someone in love with his wife and attracted to her will be less at risk of unfaithfulness. Temptations will reduce in proportion to our fascination with our spouse. The same will be true of the divine lover.

Third, I believe that having this epiphany of divine love reduces or may indeed deliver us completely from anxiety: 'When I said, "My foot is slipping," your love, O LORD, supported me. When anxiety was great within me, your consolation brought joy to my soul.'[4] Feelings of anxiety and stress are normal, but one in ten people report that they feel overwhelmed by such feelings. Yet to fall into a love affair with God can heal even some medical problems.

On the day of her baptism, a leaving student told her story to a packed church:

This is actually my last service at Aldates, so perhaps it is fitting to tell my story. Telling my testimony feels a bit like talking about somebody else. Even though I've been a

Christian for less than two years out of twenty-two, the dividing line between those two parts of my life is so great that I hardly recognise my old self.

After I left school, I had a gap year in Thailand. This was one of the loneliest times of my life. I felt a million miles away from my God and in a world where morals didn't matter. The island I was living on had the second highest rate of prostitution in the world. Of the three girls I was living with, two actively practised witchcraft and black magic, particularly on each other, and all were bullying and manipulative to each other. I met a boyfriend out there and became reliant on him for my happiness. I fell into depression and began having panic attacks. I was also consistently ill and had to take a large concoction of medication just in order to eat. I became gripped by fear and struggled with simple things like an evening out. It was from there that I entered Oxford . . . Not surprisingly, when I came to my first-year exams I had a panic attack and couldn't take them. This set off another spiral of depression and illness. I became terrified of travelling . . . I became agoraphobic, not even able to leave my house without panicking. I was put on anti-depressants, but all the time I was aware of the futility of life.

In my second year, I got to know a girl who goes to St Aldates. We began to talk about Christianity. I had a lot of issues about it, both intellectual and due to the general feeling that God had abandoned me. However, I was impressed by her humility and kindness and found myself drawn to talk to her more. She was un-pushy and gave me space to think about it. I wanted to become a Christian. During this time I became aware for the first time about my own sinful lifestyle and limitations. I went to this friend and just burst into tears. I knew she was praying over me and I wanted her to, I just cried uncontrollably. All the guilt I had, all the depression seemed to separate me so far from God. I stopped crying and she asked me if anything had changed. I felt weird, what I'd now call being under conviction. But there was one problem; I still didn't get the significance of Jesus. So she explained him to me and about his death on the cross instead of me. It was as though scales had fallen away from my eyes and ears and, although I'd heard it many times, this time I understood. I was stunned, I couldn't believe God could love me so much; it was a kind of love I didn't know how to quantify. I remember just saying, 'How can he love me so much? That's just too much.' Finally I understood. For the next two weeks I was on cloud nine.

Since I have become a Christian I have become a different person. God gave me the confidence and purpose to sort out my life. I broke up with my boyfriend, I came off anti-depressants, and I have become happy. When I first entered St Aldates Church as a Christian, I wasn't physically strong enough to stand through a whole session of worship, but God has built up my strength. That's not to say that the Christian walk of life isn't hard, but learning to follow God's will has been incredible. One of the most amazing things God did for me was to rid me of my spirit of fear . . . God's peace came over me and since that day I have never had another panic attack, and even got through finals with God's peace, which was such a victory. I could never have done it by myself.

I think the key to this lovely story is the phrase: 'I was stunned, I couldn't believe God could love me so much; it was a kind of love I didn't know how to quantify. I remember just saying, "How can he love me so much? That's just too much."' This revelation of divine love and the consequences of living in it is what I want all of us to bask in and enjoy.

Fourth, as we have seen from different epiphanies already, being a lover means you love the words that come from your lover. 'My soul faints with longing for your salvation, but I have put my hope in your word . . . Oh, how I love your law! I meditate on it all day long.'[5] When people are in love they write to each other (even if it is only text messages these days!). And they pore over those communications – often in a way that is incomprehensible to others. In the same way, lovers of God will pore over his words. John Wesley awakened to the love of God in a famous conversion moment when he felt his heart 'strangely warmed'[6]. Later he expressed his passion for the Bible in a way that I keep coming back to: 'I am a creature of a day. I am a spirit come from God, and returning to God. I want to know one thing: the way to heaven. God himself has condescended to teach me the way. He has written it down in a book. Oh, give me that book! At any price give me the book of God. Let me be a man of one book.'[7]

The fifth consequence I see is that being a lover means you are prepared to give up everything for love's sake. John, who had heard Jesus teach that 'Greater love has no one than this, that he lay down his life for his friends', passed on this insight in his letter, saying: 'This is how we know what love is: Jesus Christ laid down his life for us. And we ought to lay down our lives for our brothers.'[8]

Some years ago I wrote a book on the subject of martyrs,[9] investigating the lives of some who had been willing to pay the ultimate sacrifice of giving up their very lives for Christ and suffering martyrdom. It was interesting to see the intimate affection for him expressed by so many of them. For example, Hugh Latimer, an English bishop burnt at the stake in Oxford for the cause of the love of God, speaks movingly in his letters from prison about 'your general captain and master: Jesus Christ, the dear darling and only beloved Son of God in whom was all the Father's joy and delectation – you have him to go before you: no fairer was his way than ours, but much worse and fouler, towards the city of the heavenly Jerusalem . . .'.[10]

In fact, many martyrs seem to break through to 'bridal love' and speak of this. For example, Nicholas Ridley says he looks forward to his death at the stake in Oxford as 'the day of my wedding feast'. Nineteenth-century martyr James Hannington went to his tragic, early death on the eastern edge of Uganda singing an intimate worship song, 'Safe in the Arms of Jesus':

> Safe in the arms of Jesus,
> Safe on His gentle breast
> There by His love o'ershaded,
> Sweetly my soul shall rest.
> Hark! 'tis the voice of angels.
> Borne in a song to me,
> Over the fields of glory,
> Over the jasper sea.[11]

The sixth benefit I see is that being a lover increases one's love and compassion for lost people. In the heart of God there is a longing for lost humanity that flows down to us. It is perhaps best expressed in the famous summary: 'For God so loved the world that he gave his one and only Son, that whoever believes in him shall not perish but have eternal life . . .'[12] Love for the lost rightly flows from being a lover of God, and receiving his love. Without it we are ministering from the flesh – it smells wrong, and sooner or later it will run out. Nineteenth-century Scottish pastor Henry Drummond wrote a short meditation on love which sold twelve million copies. He called it 'The Greatest Thing in the World'. On another occasion, in an address to departing missionaries, he gave this exhortation:

> You can take nothing greater to the world than the impress and reflection of the love of God upon your own character. That is the universal language. It will take you years to speak in Chinese, or the dialects of India. From the day you land, that language of Love, understood by all, will be pouring forth in its unconscious eloquence. It is the man who is the missionary, not his words. His character is his message. In the heart of Africa, among the great Lakes, I have come across men and women who remembered the only white man they ever saw before – David Livingstone; and as you cross his footsteps in that Dark Continent, men's faces light up as they speak of the kind Doctor who passed there years ago. They could not understand him; but they felt the love that beat in his heart. Take into your new sphere of labour, where you also mean to lay down your life, that simple way of love and your lifework must succeed. You can take nothing greater, you need take nothing less. It is not worth while going if you take anything less.'[13]

Seventh, being a lover will take us in the end through personal tragedy and trial. This is so important that we have already devoted a whole chapter on 'surviving' to speak of different life experiences of the 'Great Sadness' that can overtake each of us. The psalms say: 'He will call upon me, and I will answer him; I will be with him in trouble, I will deliver him and honour him.'[14]

As a pastor, I have had to sit with people whose lives are excruciatingly hard. I have a mental picture of all those I have known who have dealt with the death of a loved one, the painful loss of a career, separation and divorce, an injury that ruins job prospects, a bankruptcy, the sickness of a child diagnosed out of the blue, some terrible unwanted news or diagnosis, an awful accident, even hellish events like the attempted suicide of a loved one. You may never have faced any of these situations, but I am certain it is important to be prepared and to have someone to whom you can turn in time of need. The very best preparation is to get to be an intimate lover of God.

Such crises disrupt life and threaten to overwhelm the people affected. It has often been said that the Chinese word for 'crisis' involves two characters: one means 'danger' and the other means 'opportunity'. The latter is sometimes difficult to see, though, when presented with the former. However, it is possible to at least hope for an understanding of the relationship between the two. Certainly the repeated message of so many of the psalms is about this need and opportunity to hold on to God in times of danger. David shows what his experience is in Psalm 116: 'The cords of death entangled me, the anguish of the grave came upon me; I was overcome by trouble and sorrow. Then I called on the name of the LORD: "O LORD, save me!" . . . when I was in great need, he saved me. Be at rest once more, O my soul, for the LORD has been good to you.' It is as if he comes through the threat of death because of God's presence and answer in darkness. The cry that goes up at midnight as 'the cords of death entangle' you is one to learn if possible in the times of relative peace.

Nearly thirty years ago, as I have said, our family's happiness was stolen away when our first and dearly loved son died in a cot death. More recently, going through pretty intense grieving in our church in Oxford, I shared with the congregation the following psalm, of which someone gave us a recording in those hard times – read by someone who really seemed to understand. In that dark season, I used to play it again and again: it somehow helped me connect with God. I had become a Christian some years earlier, after my investigations caused me to be convinced of the truth of the resurrection. I knew that heaven existed and I knew the promise of it was 'for me and my children'. But this psalm helped me to cling to and lean on the lover of my soul and thus get through that particular time of darkness. Called 'De Profundis' in *The Book of Common Prayer*, Psalm 130 says it all:

Out of the depths I cry to you, O LORD;
O Lord, hear my voice. Let your ears be attentive to my cry for mercy.
If you, O LORD, kept a record of sins, O Lord, who could stand?
But with you there is forgiveness; therefore you are feared.
I wait for the LORD, my soul waits, and in his word I put my hope.
My soul waits for the Lord more than watchmen wait for the
morning, more than watchmen wait for the morning.
O Israel, put your hope in the LORD, for with the LORD is
unfailing love and with him is full redemption.
He himself will redeem Israel from all their sins.

Being a lover helps you to hope even in the darkest times.

Eighth, and near the end of our list, being a lover will take you safely through the judgments coming upon the world. We live in a day of terrorist attacks, extreme weather and natural disaster – of earthquakes, tsunamis and nuclear accidents. In Europe, we are in the midst of a post-Christian redrawing of moral boundaries and the rise of the 'New

Atheism'. It is fair to say that the Church in the West is by and large unprepared for what is breaking upon her. But I believe she will be prepared by rediscovering a love affair with God. Currently, in the West at least, the Church is often worldly and fleshly and immature. There is no difference between her and the society around her. Tragically, she is focused on things of this world and not on the bridegroom Jesus Christ. I agree with Mike Bickle in saying: 'Because Christians are deeply rooted in the world we are unprepared to be agents of grace that the human race needs to prepare it for what is ahead.'[15]

Thus Christians find it hard to speak the right word for a situation of judgment and travail. But I believe God is beckoning to the Church. Through suffering and through times of desert, he is preparing us. (We should just add that there are notable exceptions and also that it was not ever thus!) It is comforting that Jesus said:

> There will be signs in the sun, moon and stars. On the earth, nations will be in anguish and perplexity at the roaring and tossing of the sea. Men will faint from terror, apprehensive of what is coming on the world, for the heavenly bodies will be shaken. At that time they will see the Son of Man coming in a cloud with power and great glory. When these things begin to take place, stand up and lift up your heads, because your redemption is drawing near.[16]

One might say that God's plan for the world in this overarching context is to ready a prepared 'bride', empowered for his purposes by a love affair with the bridegroom. From her sense of spiritual romance and perspective, she will view everything differently. Because she knows that the most important thing on the earth is the pleasure of loving God and people, she will have a different attitude to things, and view and respond to events happening through a lens of the love.

Ninth, and on the same theme, being a lover will cause us to grow in prophetic insight. It is in the place of worship, when we are lost in wonder before an open heaven, that God speaks a prophetic word. That is to say, he reveals his compassionate love and mercy. How we need true words from heaven in our generation! The one who loves God will stay close to him and rise early to listen, like the one spoken of by the prophet Isaiah: 'The Sovereign LORD has given me an instructed tongue, to know the word that sustains the weary. He wakens me morning by morning, wakens my ear to listen like one being taught.'[17] It is in the place of early seeking that the lover of God gets insight and can receive a true word to help instead of hinder. Somewhat akin to John the Baptist's role as forerunner of Christ, the lover of God may

> be called a prophet of the Most High; for you will go on before the Lord to prepare the way for him, to give his people the knowledge of salvation through the forgiveness of their sins, because of the tender mercy of our God, by which the rising sun will come to us from heaven to shine on those living in darkness and in the shadow of death, to guide our feet into the path of peace.[18]

And last but not least in this list of benefits, I want to add a note of caution. Being a lover may go to your head, so in entering this way of life, we have an increased need for accountability, for the testing of prophecy or prophetic lifestyle to keep our feet on the ground and to be connected to reality. By definition, this – like the challenge of discerning right directions in any love affair – is a heady business. Paul provides common-sense rules of engagement for testing prophecy and working things out in the context of community which we need to be aware of today if we are to avoid repeating ancient heresies (or finding new ones of our own). For example the Montanists (c. fourth century) and Quakers (c. seventeenth century) and Irvingites (c. nineteenth century) all started well with a desire for a return to book of Acts experiences of God. They were keen on visions and prophecy. But in seeking a special light or revelation, they ended up separating from the mainstream Church into extremes of behaviour and practice.

A commitment to church community is an essential outworking of our 'soul-resting'. We must learn to 'test everything' and lean on one another rather than being aloof and independent, and in so doing we may hope to steer clear of some of those schisms and heresies that have so often been the badge of the Church in the past. Most of all, we must learn to lean on the Lover of our souls, and his Word, and not on our own wisdom.

As we learn to rest in the Father's love, and the bridal love for Christ, burnout, temptation and anxiety will all reduce. A love for the Word will grow, as will love for people. The ability to live sacrificially, the capacity to survive suffering and the crises breaking on the world and the capacity to live prophetic and hopeful lives: all of this will flow from abiding, resting and remaining in the love of God.

Collect for Resting

Lord Jesus Christ, darling of heaven who took on your own shoulders the burden of our sin and restless existence: grant that in humility we may hear your call to lean upon your breast, that out of this place of loving rest we might show you to the world. Amen.

The whole day I felt like a hungry ghost: hungry for
attention and affection. I ended up angry, not just at
those who didn't give me what I craved but at my own
spirit for being so needy . . . feeling abandoned,
rejected, forgotten . . .
Henri J. M. Nouwen, *Sabbatical Journey*

And then I felt sad because I realized that once people
are broken in certain ways, they can't ever be fixed, and
this is something nobody ever tells you when you are
young and it never fails to surprise you as you grow
older as you see the people in your life break one by
one. You wonder when your turn is going to be, or if
it's already happened.
Douglas Coupland, *Life After God*

Catch for us the foxes, the little foxes that ruin the vineyards,
our vineyards that are in bloom.
Song of Songs 2:15

CHAPTER ELEVEN

Healing

My children sometimes joke with me that I would like to have a massive banner inside our church building greeting people as they walk in, proclaiming: 'Feel the Love!' But I haven't yet. I don't know if it is the fact that it would be uncool or presumptuous that restrains me. Recently I was moved by the pink neon artwork sign hung under the huge stained-glass windows of Liverpool Cathedral by the British artist Tracey Emin, which read: '*I felt you and I knew you loved me*'. There is a hunger for love. And yet do we actually believe that we are loved by God and receive his love?

Alienation, loneliness and disintegration are so prevalent throughout our world today. There are so many broken marriages and relationships, so many people who have not been faithful to the love they once promised, so many children in revolt against their parents.

I believe part of the call to love God is also to receive love personally from God. Jesus implies the importance of allowing ourselves to be loved when he reminds his disciples to love their neighbour as themselves. Unfortunately, often the last person we will give our attention to caring for is ourselves. Often things are pushed below the surface until in the end there will be some kind of relational meltdown or depression. The bride of the Song of Songs laments: '[They] made me take care of the vineyards: my own vineyard I have neglected!'[1] It is good to ask God to plough, replant, weed, prune and thus restore our own personal landscape and history. We do this not simply in order better to love others, but also because if he loves us, we would miss the mark badly if we refused to receive his love. Like a bride who keeps constantly cooking and cleaning, but will not take time to be loved and to love, we would miss the point – and end up ruining the relationship.

I want to admit that there was a time when I found it hard to believe and receive the love of God and, as a result, I often did not live lovingly. As a leader I instead put pressure on others to do what I wanted. Many reading this, from all kinds of professions, may identify with this inner fear of failure. We compensate for this, which can lead to needless striving, overwork, controlling behaviour, and anything and everything other than joy. In the past, I may have had vision, it is true, but I have not been at rest in it. I have glimpsed the church community's calling to be a deep joy in the city. But I have been striving in my own strength, and wrongly controlling people to make it happen: I have not been a joy but a fear.

This came to a head for me some years ago in Paris, where we lived for ten years, serving in a French-speaking church in inner-city Belleville, at the heart of the capital. A Swiss pastor friend was a colleague in the same church. One day he did not come to a meeting I was hosting. My reaction was shame, regret, and fear that he might leave the church. I called a meeting with him and let him know of my disapproval and distress. He calmly said: 'Charlie, why do you get like that, and what is going on inside you that brings such fear and control?' He was an experienced counsellor who had himself suffered and been divorced. He was broken and open and he had nothing to prove. Nor was he intimidated by me.

Gradually he helped me over a period of time to ask the question: What is going on?

Shortly after the first incident, the same anger and frustration arose again when I became irritated with an unsuspecting member of the church for wanting to give too lengthy a notice that was not part of my plan (sad but true!). My reaction was such as to lead to a breakdown in relationship with the man in question (though he was himself a troubled man), which alerted me to look beneath the surface. I began to ask myself: Why? What did I fear? What was I ashamed of that led me to control others and get tense and fearful if things went wrong? I wanted to love God and love people, but I could switch suddenly to being paranoid about failure, and therefore fail to love people at all.

I was emotionally unhealthy but I had not recognised it and did not know what to do about it. Emotional health is a big topic today. Counselling programmes or life-skills forums are set up to address it. One such, the Landmark Forum, describes one part of the training it offers in this way: 'In this section we are given a technology for putting the past where it belongs – in the past. We begin to design our lives as a free and authentic expression – from what is possible, rather than what has been. Unencumbered by the past, we experience a greater level of vitality, well-being and fun, and are able to enjoy a newfound sense of connection and intimacy with the people in our lives.'[2]

Many programmes offer a similar kind of 'technology for putting the past where it belongs'. And yet the word 'technology' is lacking when in fact it is 'the technician' we need. It is an encounter with Christ, the author of history – our history – that will heal. He is the only one equipped and able to deliver this, as we come to him!

Our past, whatever 'technology' we might employ, is always liable to invade our present and ruin our future. Regarding my experiences in Paris, when I looked beneath the surface into my past, I realised it was not too hard to see a pattern. My parents had divorced when I was fourteen. Out of the blue, my world had crashed down around me, never to be the same again. Then, when I was thirty, our first son died in a cot death. I have already commented on this event, which was sudden, without warning, and subsequently drained all the colour out of our world in a way we had no idea how to deal with. We hardly knew how to survive in our marriage. But thankfully we came closer rather than being driven apart, unlike so many couples who suffer the loss of a child. There is much more one could say about the challenges of navigating through such times.[3]

It was not difficult to see a pattern of past pain which led me into a fear of abandonment should anything unexpected happen. Recognising this and talking it through carefully with my friend was a big part of my healing. At the same time I received some prayer that my ruined foundations would be restored and rebuilt, and that I would be delivered from three negative reactions: shame, fear and wrongful control. These three are a package of reflexes which are all present at the fall, back in the book of Genesis. Adam and Eve have been found out. They feel devastated. They are ashamed, they are afraid, and they try to control the consequences by hiding themselves. And so begins the sad litany of countless similar reactions experienced by you, me and everyone in history when things go wrong in our lives. Shame, fear, control are so often substituted for love. This is so common I sometimes think there should be a new Myers-Briggs personality category to add to ESTJ, etc., namely CB – to stand for 'Controlling Bully'.[4]

The good news is that God through Christ comes to seek and to save that which was lost. As well as 'lost souls' per se, this also encompasses our lost humanness, the alienation between man and God, man and woman, between parents and children, brothers and sisters, man and the environment and throughout creation. The Son of God comes and pays the agonising price – so that by his wounds, we are made whole. In our deep subconscious we feel shame, we feel guilt, and we know there is payment needed. Some push this under the surface, revolting against what their conscience whispers to them. But if we are truthful we will know that there is a cost to be paid. The deep glory of the Christian message is that God so loved humankind that when the time had fully come, he moved into the world in order to pay the costly debt in Christ instead of us. He substituted himself to pay what we ought to pay. Somehow, then, as we apply his loving and powerful act of sacrifice to our lives, he takes our sin and all our bad stuff. We are restored, delivered, renewed, filled and we become new people. We discover we are children of God and hence his co-heirs. We have nothing to prove. This in itself is a joy and a delight. It is an important key. And, God willing, it will lead to us becoming a joy and a delight for others.

If we know this in our hearts and not just our heads, then we can ourselves become a source of joy in our situation. I can testify, in that Parisian spring, the simple act of talking it through was like an epiphany of relief that the winter was over. The old, exhausting round of shame, fear and control was broken. I was a receiver of joy in the soul. Once you know this secret, you can show many the way to it. It is contagious and compelling. We are called to be lovers. But first we must go into the painful areas of our past and know the love of God there. We must receive healing for ourselves, deeply and in a lasting manner, before we can enter our destiny to pass it on to others.

Dutch spiritual writer Henri Nouwen was able to connect to so many, perhaps partly because of his being so open about his insecurities and sense of weakness or brokenness. In his last book, *Sabbatical Journey*, he concludes: 'I am increasingly convinced that it is possible to live the wounds of the past not as gaping abysses that cannot be fulfilled and therefore keep threatening us but as gateways to new life.'[5] Because of our brokenness, we may need to apply this daily and with real effort for the rest of our lives. Many feel uncertain and find they have developed a kind of Achilles' heel in this area, so need daily doses of realisation of the constant covenant love and good intentions of God for them.

In the Song of Songs, we read God as lover saying: 'My dove in the clefts of the rock, in the hiding-places on the mountainside, show me your face, let me hear your voice; for your voice is sweet, and your face is lovely.'[6]

Hear God saying this to you. He wants you to lift your face and love him. He wants you to express your affection – he wants to hear your voice. The passage continues: 'Catch for us the foxes, the little foxes that ruin the vineyards, our vineyards that are in bloom.'

This is exactly what is needed if we are to live as lovers. Little foxes from the past, habits of shame and fear and control, need to be identified and caught. We need to dare actually to believe in God's love for us. It is a covenant love. This is a deep idea but has to do with the fact that we are each chosen and adopted as sons and daughters and hence as heirs. That is to say, we have an unassailable future in the benevolent plans of God. This is very good news, not just in theory but in practice: it can move us from darkness into light, from loathing ourselves into loving ourselves and then loving our neighbours as ourselves. The bride in the Song goes on to give permission to Christ to come right in and 'browse' through all her history until all the shadows of disappointment and the darkness of the past are healed and the last shadows flee: 'My lover is mine and I am his; he browses among the lilies. Until the day breaks and the shadows flee . . .'[7]

If we take care of our own vineyard we will be able to take care of others. The one who comes in openness and broken-ness to Christ in this way finds rest for their soul. Jesus said that person is then free to 'learn of him'. The main thing they will learn is the unforced rhythm and privilege of loving others as themselves. They will begin to love freely and give love away. The result of this will be joy!

This healing from the past brings us into a life lived in the reality of God's covenant love. I wonder if you have had this epiphany? Have you received the love of God so deeply that you end up saying: 'This is too good to be true! How can this be? How can he love me that much?' Many, many stories can be told of those who have been granted this understand-ing. As discussed earlier, I believe Moses 'sees' it when he asks: 'Show me your glory.' He understands God's *hesed* covenant love for humankind. Towards the end of his life on earth, Jesus, having known it continually through his life, has come to the time to pass it on, and prays 'that the love you have for me may be in them'[8]. John acknowledges it: 'We love because he first loved us.'[9] Paul prays for the Ephesians to 'know this love'.[10]

C.S. Lewis refers to this process of becoming alert to the healing love of God as being 'more like when a man, after long sleep, still lying motionless in bed, becomes aware that he is now awake'. This awareness of awakening can happen after recognising Christ, at the moment of decision, or over a period of years. When God drew C.S. Lewis to himself, there was a time when he became conscious of his own sinfulness. 'For the first time I examined myself with a seriously practical purpose,' wrote Lewis. 'And there I found what appalled me: a zoo of lusts, a bedlam of ambitions, a nursery of fears, a harem of fondled hatreds. My name is legion.' Though Lewis was frightened by what he saw in himself, the Holy Spirit would open his heart and mind to Christ's forgiveness and love. It was on 22 September 1931 that Lewis said yes. According to his testimony, this happened on a ride to Whipsnade Zoo with his brother Warren. Lewis tells about it in his book *Surprised by Joy*:

> I know very well when, but hardly how, the final step was taken. I was driven to Whipsnade one sunny morning. When we set out I did not believe that Jesus Christ is the Son of God, and when we reached the zoo I did. Yet I had not exactly spent the journey in thought. Nor in great emotion . . . It was more like when a man, after long sleep, still lying motionless in bed, becomes aware that he is now awake.[11]

Personally, since my experience of this awakening, I try to live each day with a sense of the unrelenting benevolence of God for me and for my house. If I fall back into fear, I check myself and follow David's example in saying something like: 'Hey, why are you so disquieted, O my soul? Hope in God!' I endeavour to take myself back into the reality of God's covenant. Sometimes my success is greater than at other times, but nonetheless it is a choice we can make to accept that 'God is for us'.

In the process of deliverance and healing, it is good to feed on the manna which is the Word of God – the bread which can sustain us each day. We may meditate on passages which pour out truth about the love of God. To take just one example, in writing to the Ephesians Paul lays out a seven-fold richness to receiving the love of God. He is writing to a community who are in danger, as I fear we are, of losing their first love. He says that they (and he) have been blessed with 'every spiritual blessing in Christ', offering them an epiphany that if rightly received can lead to healing and freedom. Instead of living in fear of curses and failure, believers in Christ can face each day with confidence. We can daily celebrate the fact that we are chosen to be blameless; adopted as children; redeemed (released from prisons); forgiven; given to understand God's will for the future of the world; chosen to live for his praise; and sealed with the Holy Spirit.

Ephesians 1: a theological basis for a life of love

Paul begins with our destiny from God: 'he chose us in him . . . to be holy and blameless.' Shame is not to be our experience, but freedom. Second, because of love, we are chosen 'to be adopted as his sons through Jesus Christ'. We are to be and can live like heirs – children of the family of God – with a security and a confidence that therefore all will be well. Third, we are set free ('in him we have redemption though his blood') from any prisons we may have been put in by circumstances, or put ourselves in. He paid the ransom, if we will accept it, so we can walk tall and free. Fourth, we have 'the forgiveness of sins' – this should also be understood as reconciliation of the heart with our Father, a sense of close-ness you only get within the family. It is like when a rebellious or estranged child comes home to stay: rest comes to the family again as unity and peace flow together and forgiveness imbues the atmosphere of the household.

Fifth, as family members he lets us see his will. Many are the quarrels between families over surprising revelations when the 'last will and testament' of a parent is read out. But God makes known to us 'the mystery of his will'. This is also a motivator for love, as we understand 'his good pleasure . . . when the times will have reached their fulfilment – to bring all things together under one head, even Christ'. This plan extends beyond the mere salvation of humanity to embrace all things in heaven and earth – the entire universe. The entire universe was brought into chaos and conflict,[12] but at the climax he has chosen, God will bring all things into unity and make them subject to Christ. Jesus Christ will then be ruler of the entire universe! There is no way we could know that such a plan existed if God had not revealed it to us. This understanding helps us and spurs us on to live loving lives.

Sixth, we understand our purpose in life, namely to be 'to the praise of his glory'. We are called to be worshippers first, workers second. We can understand the power of praise and worship as we forget ourselves and acknowledge him daily. In addition, our working lives certainly can be a constant development of that relationship of worship to God, whatever task we are engaged in.

Seventh and finally, Paul concludes, we are sealed with the promised Holy Spirit, who guarantees that all of this is true. This mysterious 'sealing' is vital for our life of love. As we invite the love of God, the power of God in the Holy Spirit to come upon our lives, he does many deep works. Among these, he confirms in us that we are children of God. In addition, he will give us power to be witnesses, filled to overflowing with the very love of God in our actions.[13]

If we get hold of this, we have come a long way. We have come to him; we will experience the benefits of abiding. We may well find ourselves straining to see God enable this love to be passed on to others and not kept to ourselves. I believe we will then be becoming a people of prayer.

Collect for St Luke the Evangelist – A Collect for Healing
Almighty God, who called Luke the physician, whose praise is in the gospel, to be an evangelist and physician of the soul: may it please you, that by the wholesome medicines of the doctrine delivered by him, all the diseases of our souls may be healed; through the merits of your Son Jesus Christ our Lord.

God says to His own Son: 'Ask of me and I will give you the nations for your inheritance.' If the royal and divine Son cannot be exempted from the rule of asking that he may have, you and I cannot expect the rule to be relaxed in our favour. God will bless Elijah and send rain, but Elijah must pray for it. If the chosen nation is to prosper, Samuel must plead for it. If the Jews are to be delivered, Esther must intercede. God will bless Paul and the nations shall be converted through him, but Paul must pray . . .

C.H. Spurgeon

You do not have, because you do not ask God.

James 4:2

CHAPTER TWELVE

Asking

If we see him, if we are given an epiphany, however brief or veiled, of heaven open, then a love for prayer is often miraculously born. As we have seen, union and communion is our privilege as we learn the secret of abiding in him. Then, as people see him, they will have different reactions – to fall at his feet as though dead like John, to worship and rest in his presence as Moses did, or to repent in dust and ashes like Job. But no discussion of epiphanies would be complete without noting that Jesus wants to draw us into the mystery of asking.

At this time, when history needs the voice of love, it is clear to me that we need prophets of transformation who will give out of God's love to the hungry of the world who knock on our door. We need Wilberforces, Shaftesburys, Mother Teresas. But I believe the prophetic voice of love in the twenty-first century will be born out of the place of prayer. Asking will precede transformation. Intervention flows from intercession. Strategy will be revealed in the prayer rooms of Britain. But where are those prayer rooms? And who is in them?

The fact is that there are already the beginnings of a hopeful movement of women and men who have felt Eliot's 'drawing of His love and the voice of His calling'[1] into the prayer room, the place of prayer where the presence of God is to be found. Those who love God have always prayed, of course. The Church was born in a 24/7 prayer environment of all-together-in-one-place constant prayer until, fifty days later, Pentecost happened. But this did not bring a stop to the seeking. Rather the reverse: the early Church certainly knew how to love God through prayer.

Jesus, with a whip of rope, cleared out the Temple of its restrictive culture and rebuked its leaders for robbing people of their blood-bought heritage of connecting with God. What he built afterwards throughout the world could (and perhaps should) have been called 'houses of prayer' instead of 'churches'.

At times of awakening, God has always acted by first drawing people into a renewal of prayer. The history of the Church is arguably a history of prayer awakenings. Whether it is John on Patmos, Paul in prison, the church in Antioch, you see this asking – for God's power and action – everywhere in the biblical Church. After that, the continuing early accounts of the Church often show a people at prayer, connected to God through asking. The martyr Polycarp, who had known the apostle John personally, delayed his own burning by an articulate two-hour-long prayer that converted the soldiers who came to arrest him.[2] In the fourth and fifth centuries, Augustine and the early leaders of the Church likewise knew how to pray, saying: 'Holy prayer is the column of all virtues; a ladder to God . . . the foundation of faith . . . What can be more excellent than prayer; what is more profitable to our life; what sweeter to our souls; what more sublime, in the course of our whole life, than the practice of prayer!'[3]

Around the same time, the Desert Fathers retreated into the lonely wilderness in order better to advance the kingdom, and as such they are a parable of example in our noisy times. In the tenth century, Bernard de Clairvaux instituted a company of pray-ers in medieval France. At the sixteenth-century Reformation, the same prayer awakening was there, substantially preceding everything that then happened. Martin Luther said: I have so much to do that if I didn't spend at least three hours a day in prayer I would never get it all done.' He wrote:

> That the Holy Scriptures cannot be penetrated by study and talent is most certain. Therefore your first duty is to begin to pray, and to pray to this effect that if it please God to accomplish something for His glory – not for yours or any other person's – He very graciously grant you a true understanding of His words . . . You must, therefore, completely despair of your own industry and ability and rely solely on the inspiration of the Spirit.[4]

The eighteenth-century Great Awakening was preceded by a famous prayer meeting in Herrnhut, Moravia, that lasted 100 years. This has been the ancient calling of monasteries and contemplatives throughout the world and throughout twenty centuries of Christian history: to ensure the incense of prayer and worship never stops ascending to heaven. The encouraging miracle is that since the 1990s, there has been what can only be called a 'prayer awakening' throughout the world.[5]

I believe the 24-7 Prayer movement – and other similar moves of God – are part of an awakening of love for God. Young people in particular seem to understand the pleasures of loving God and waiting on him. This is a miracle that only God can do: to raise up a generation that will love to seek his face and spend time with him, because they have tasted and seen that the Lord is good. I emailed a few of the undergraduate students in our church asking why it is that they love the place of prayer – and was surprised at the speed with which I had replies:

'There is nothing more precious, more full of love, and more incredible than falling on my knees and crying out to God in prayer. It is there, in those moments, where I rest in God's presence and put aside everything else, that I feel complete.'

'Prayer is so much more than words, it is the driving force behind movements of God, casting out evil and releasing the lavish grace God has for us. Prayer is a lifetime calling full of learning and challenges, but one that will never disappoint and is always worthwhile.'

'God has taught me patience; to wait on him truly renews one's strength. I am encouraged not to give up on prayer, and how thankful am I that God has answered me.'

'In prayer, God breaks through me. He tears down my barriers, fights through my mask, and he moulds me into his image, shapes my will to his . . . Prayer makes my heart vulnerable to God, so that he can place on it whatever he wishes.'

'The place of prayer is exciting because it's the place where God changes me most. Prayer connects us to the bigger story, God's story of his plan for our world. Even the most trivial and mundane things can take on eternal significance when we offer them to God in prayer.'

'I love the place of prayer because I know that when one person honestly seeks God with everything, he will find him, and he will find him not just for himself but for many. And therefore I love this movement because I believe that as we corporately fall on our faces in the place of prayer we can find God for an entire generation!'

'I'm coming to learn about the importance of the place of prayer as a stage of preparation. I keep returning to the beginning of 1 Samuel because it's so sweet; the picture of Samuel who grew up in the house of God, and was in his very presence all his life, and yet who, as late as chapter 3, had still never heard the voice of the Lord, but was simply in the Temple being precious unto him . . . and then when God did speak, the rest is history!'

'I guess I would say I love the place of prayer because it's where I am most myself.'

'The Christian is the child of the King whose doors are always open. At his throne through our cries, our petitions and our groaning prayers we fight for the in-breaking of the reign of God whose government will be upheld with justice . . . All prayer is set in front of the horizon of the final victory where the cross is centre stage.'

These saints in their early twenties are part of a worldwide movement of God – 24-7 Prayer,[6] International Houses of Prayer,[7] Prayer Rooms – anywhere and everywhere. Our own community in Oxford recently knocked down and rebuilt an old ruin, and in its basement renovated and opened a 'Catacombs Prayer Room' to be available to the Christians of Oxford simply for unceasing prayer at the heart of our city, and which we plan to open 24/7 eventually.[8]

If we look away from the West to Africa, Asia and South America, we find much prayer and a greater burden, intensity and love for God through prayer. In these continents, we find stadia used for all-night prayer, beaches filled with people joining in prayer, prayer mountains, prayer towers, prayer caves. All over China, spaces are being set up to gather people who know how to love God through prayer. Some in China have a particular burden that the Chinese should take the gospel all along the ancient silk road through the poorest and least evangelised countries of the world, all the way 'Back to Jerusalem'.[9] These are examples of creative missionary prayer initiatives set up to love God and ask him for his kingdom to come.

What kind of prayer do we need? Paul speaks of 'all kinds of prayer': we could think of groaning prayer, weeping prayer, intelligent prayer, biblical prayer, prayer which stands in the gap, prayer with faith, hopeful prayer, prayer for an outpouring, long-obedience-in-the-same-direction prayer, quiet prayer, silent prayer, repentant prayer. We need All-Prayer. We need to become a house of prayer, taking back ground from the den of thieves who are robbing our land of its history and destiny.

We may feel this is true, but might wonder: How do I begin? We may have felt a stirring to this kind of deep love in the past, but now it has got buried. How do I come back to my first love? Some of us are perplexed by prayer and feel sleepy as soon as it is mentioned. Or we feel intimidated, put off by the intensity of some who pray. We feel excluded by a culture that is not ours, and we fear perhaps never will be.

If that is your experience, I urge you to plead with God for the door of prayer to open to you. We are not looking for Christian subculture prayer, but to discover biblical prayer as Christ asked for it, and connection with him. The fact is that to be a Christian without prayer is like having a marriage without love – almost impossible! But a Christian with prayer can do almost everything. E.M. Bounds said: 'Few Christians have anything but a vague idea of the power of prayer. The Church seems almost wholly unaware of the power God puts into her hands. To graduate in the school of prayer is to master the whole course of religious life.'[10]

I would say that if we want to test the level of our love for God, a good gauge may be our commitment to prayer. Jesus said that if we love him we will keep his commandments, one of which, repeated again and again, is to 'ask'. I think the reason for this is that our level of asking shows our level of dependence. Another way Jesus puts it is that we 'abide', or 'remain' attached to the vine and so bear the fruit of love. In case we don't understand how to do that, he adds, 'If you remain in me and my words remain in you, ask whatever you wish, and it will be given to you. This is to my Father's glory, that you bear much fruit.'[11]

To double-check we have understood the link between the fruit of love and asking, he sums up: 'I chose you and appointed you to go and bear fruit – fruit that will last. Then the Father will give you whatever you ask in my name. This is my command: Love each other.'[12] In this way, Jesus challenges us to regularity, commitment, enjoyment and experiences of God in the place of abiding and asking prayer. Yet so many of us are tongue-tied, silent, mute and empty in the place of prayer. This is less so in the global South, and in Asia, but overwhelmingly so in the West. There seems to be a deafening silence.

In 2011, the film *The King's Speech* picked up a string of awards. People identified with the vulnerability of George VI, who could not speak out in public but so much needed to. A stammering son of a king was helped to find out how to speak at a time of great need. It is interesting that George VI used his voice prophetically. First he called people to trust in God. In his Christmas Day broadcast of 1939, he quotes a poem: 'I said to the man who stood at the Gate of the Year, "Give me a light that I may tread safely into the unknown." And he replied, "Go out into the darkness, and put your hand into the Hand of God. That shall be better than light, and safer than a known way."' This was inspired communication as darkness fell on Europe. But it did not end there. The king later used this renewed voice of his to call the whole nation to prayer. At the time of the D-Day landings, which would bring the beginning of the end to six years of cruel war, his words were published in national newspapers on 7 June 1944[13] entitled 'the King's Call to Prayer':

> That we may be worthily matched with this new summons to destiny, I desire solemnly to call my people to prayer and dedication ... I hope that throughout the present crisis of the liberation of Europe there may be offered up earnest, continuous and widespread prayer. If from every place of worship, from every home and factory, men and women of all ages and many races and occupations, prayers and inter-cessions rise, then please God ... the predictions of an ancient psalm may be fulfilled: 'The Lord will give strength to his people: the Lord will give his people the blessing of peace.'

I guess there had been an epiphany for the king to realise the urgency of using all means to find his voice. But in the end, the stammer was overcome, a voice was found – and a message to go with it.

In a way the same thing happens for Esther in the Bible. It is left to her uncle Mordecai to supply her with her epiphanic wake-up call: 'Who knows but that you have come to royal position for such a time as this?' So it is that she awakes from intimidation and silence and says: 'I will go in to the king and if I perish, I perish.' It is for us a picture of intercessory, petitionary, pleading prayer: to go in to the king and make our request known.

In the same way, epiphany awakening, perhaps helped by

coaching from others, will bring us into finding our voice and help us to develop a vocabulary of prayer.

The idea of asking is not too difficult to grasp, but evidently Jesus understands it is something we will struggle with. And so he reinforces the principle of asking with images and stories. To the friend at midnight and the hard-hearted judge, Jesus adds stories of the son asking for a fish or an egg, and the father who likes giving presents.

If we lack wisdom, James tells us in his letter we must ask for it. The apostle then clarifies: 'You cannot have what you want . . . You do not have, because you do not ask God', adding as a helpful afterthought: 'You do not receive, because you ask with wrong motives, that you may spend what you get on your pleasures.'[14]

So how do we journey back, towards becoming a house of prayer for the sake of love?

As usual, there are various keys offered to us. Two obvious ones are that we must learn the basics, and practise what we learn. But these alone are not enough. If you want to become a master musician, there will be technical lessons combined with persistent practice, but without inspiration it will not happen. In this call to become people who ask, we will need inspiration. Inspiration is sometimes like contagion. To catch flu, you need to be in the company of people who have the virus. In a more positive way, I have found it helpful to get into the company of those who pray. This may mean crossing cities or even continents to experience the atmosphere of an African, South American or Asian prayer gathering and be infected by it and bring it home. It is worth it. A concert violinist would not hesitate to make such a journey and such an investment to enhance their playing. I am not talking about becoming a conference groupie or spiritual tourist, but seeking God and the godly. Sometimes spiritual things require an urgent seeking. Elisha wanted a double portion of Elijah's spirit. This required him not to take his eyes off his master. In the end his energetic, consistent asking was rewarded. 'The spirit of Elijah was resting on Elisha.'[15]

Of course, the one whose company we most aspire to sit in is that of the Lord Jesus himself and it is our daily privilege to go to him directly. We have seen how to begin with this great task. As I write now I am aware of his presence. I have quietened my heart and am still. There is quiet music that is God-directed. I know he is here. Is this artificial, or to take the name of the Lord in vain? I trust not. He himself said: 'I am with you always.'[16] His prayer is for me to be with him where he is so that I may see his glory.[17] And yet often I miss this in the busy press of distractedness. The thorns of life's worries, riches, pleasures choke the life out of me, as Jesus predicted.[18]

A.W. Tozer said this: 'Christ is every man's contemporary. His presence and His power are offered to us at this time of mad activity and mechanical noises as certainly as to fishermen on the quiet lake of Galilee . . . The only condition is that we get still enough to hear His voice and that we believe and heed what we hear.'[19] The need for daily stillness and seeking is non-negotiable in the school of learning to ask.

Another key already mentioned is practice: perhaps a bit like the five-finger exercises engaged in by those learning an instrument. But instead I suggest we learn the spiritual exercises of ancient giants of prayer in the Bible.

With this in mind, some time ago I spent a year researching and writing on the mysterious godly adventures of nation-changing men and women in the Bible. I wanted to learn their 'exercises' in so far as this is possible. This came out in the form of a book called *The Discipline of Intimacy*.[20] There is intimacy, and there is also a need for discipline. Looking at Jesus, the discipline of prayer was helpful, practical and life-transforming. At the same time, looking at Hannah, Esther and others, I noted that 'the destiny of nations is not in the hands of the multi-nationals or governments or politicians but in the hands of the people of God who pray'. I still believe this today.[21] One of the nation-changers and lovers of God I did not include in that earlier book was Moses. But it is his adventure with God that I can't get away from now. It can inspire us all as we look at his pattern for loving prayer today.

Moses had an encounter with God that brought a whole people out of slavery – yet his challenge was that halfway through their journey into destiny and the Promised Land, they seemed worse off than at the beginning. It had started well, but at what should have been their half-time opportunity for recuperation in the journey to recovery, the people were dancing round an idolatrous golden calf (a false god). Things were unravelling in an addictive display of idolatrous lifestyle that would lead to chaos. What is more, they denied all responsibility, with Aaron saying: 'They gave me the gold, and I threw it into the fire . . . and out came this calf!'[22]

If we are honest, one of our obstacles to asking is hopelessness. We often sense a gathering darkness when looking at our nation, our city, our friends, even our family. What started well can seem to be unravelling, as with Moses. Those nearest to us can seem to be deadened to all thought of God and our nation can seem to be sleepwalking into chaos. What do we do when our lives feel barren in terms of the need for real loving transformation of our land?

As an answer to this, I recommend the four prayers of Moses noted in an earlier chapter.[23] Faced with general chaos and a golden calf, he does not give up. He does not stop holding on to God. He does not step back but steps up and stands in the gap as someone who will not let go of the promises of God. His prayers can be ours today.

Teach me your ways that I may know you

God's ways are not our ways and thus are often such a challenge to our comfort zone. For while our goal in life may be to become self-sufficient, his goal is to help us to learn to lean. Speaking of a time of great hardship when he nearly despaired of life itself, Paul says, 'This happened so that we might not rely on ourselves, but God who raises the dead.' The ways of God are to be found in the Word of God, so as we pray, we should let our prayer be led and breathed into by the Word of God in the Bible. This prayer is asking to become an expert in the Word of God – to become one who meditates daily on the ways of God in the Word of God, in order to 'know our God and be strong and do exploits'.[24]

Remember this nation is your people

Moses had a whole people group on his heart – and so do I. I have a dream that one day in the UK (and in mainland Europe, for that matter) revival will come to our land and that a new reformation will come from heaven. I believe we can pray like Moses: 'Lord, remember this nation.' This will require us to be students of what God has done in our country, as well as knowing his ways with nations.[25] For example, into the very floor of the central lobby of the Houses of Parliament is inscribed the text: 'Unless the LORD builds the house, its builders labour in vain.'[26] We can pray:

'Remember this nation is your people.' In nearly every nation under the sun there are martyr stories we can rehearse before God, like Bishop Hannington's last words as he was martyred on the road to Uganda: 'Tell the king I die for Uganda. I have bought this road with my blood.' Into the University of Oxford's DNA is written the Latin motto: '*Dominus Illumination Mea*' (The Lord is my Light). We can pray: 'Remember this university is your people.' We are called in prayer to unblock wells of the past and wherever we are, whatever our constituency, I believe this is part of how to do so.

Let your presence go with us

The presence of God is something that I am asking for. Though this is a mystery, I want to do all I can to draw and attract the presence of God. This may involve us in a journey of humility, holiness, hungering after God. It may involve pursuing justice and serving the poor. Always it will require unity with other Christians, for 'there the Lord commanded the blessing'.[27] As we pray this, we need to be prepared for deep reconciliation with people from whom we may have formerly been divided, if we are to take this seriously, so as to be prepared for God's presence. The asking Christian will love, long for, covet, recognise and not be satisfied without the presence of God.

Now show me your glory

All my Christian life I have been drawn by the thought and reality of the glory of God. Epiphany moments throughout the Bible and church history beckon us: God, it seems, waits to be wanted. And Jesus' prayer in John 17 suggests it is to be our destiny: 'Father, I want those you have given me to be with me where I am, and to see my glory.'[28] I believe it comes through longing, suffering, waiting, asking . . . but it will come.

Collect for Asking (Cranmer's Collect for the Third Sunday after Trinity)

Lord, we beseech thee mercifully to hear us, and unto us whom thou hast given a hearty desire to pray, grant that by thy mighty aid we may be defended; through Jesus Christ our Lord. Amen.

PART III: GO

The third part of this exploration of epiphanies turns our gaze outwards. We have come and seen. We have learnt the place of abiding. Now it is time to go. But we should note that the act of going may also have its epiphanies. And as the love of God begins to heal us and restore us, we will begin the hopeful task of living for others.

Peace be with you! As the Father has sent me, I am sending you . . .
John 20:21

I believe that we are not real social workers. We may be
doing social work in the eyes of the people, but we are
really contemplatives in the heart of the world. For we
are touching the Body of Christ twenty-four hours. We
have twenty-four hours in his presence, and so you and
I . . . There is so much suffering, so much hatred, so
much misery, and we with our prayer, with our
sacrifice, are beginning at home. Love begins at home,
and it is not how much we do, but how much love we
put in the action that we do. It is to God Almighty
– how much we do it does not matter, because He is
infinite, but how much love we put in that action. How
much we do to Him in the person that we are serving.
Mother Teresa's Nobel Lecture, 11 December 1979

For I was hungry and you gave me something to eat, I
was thirsty and you gave me something to drink, I was
a stranger and you invited me in, I needed clothes and
you clothed me, I was sick and you looked after me, I
was in prison and you came to visit me.
Matthew 25:35–36

CHAPTER THIRTEEN

Touching: Serving the poor

As we get going in this lifestyle of love, it is encouraging to know that those who live for others are a source of happiness and the love of God in our land. When we meet those who live this life-for-others, we are glad, for they bring with them joy and delight.

Before he was born, it was said of the greatest of all prophets, John the Baptist, that he would be a joy and a delight. Sometimes, when we have enjoyed fellowship with people, my wife will say to me: 'Aren't they a joy to be with?' Sometimes – in a church or community or your own family – you meet people who are caring, generous, thoughtful and unflinchingly loyal. They are a joy and a delight. We need more of them. The world is better for them. The big question is: Am I one of them? Am I a joy and a delight to others, because I have been with Jesus, and his transforming love is actually transforming me?

Those who are a joy and a delight, I think, will be those who are full of life and love. They are concerned for others, not self-absorbed. They do not try to push you into their plan. They are open-handed and helpful. They express interest without being intrusive; offer affection without manipulation; give advice without pressure. They express encouragement easily, generously. They look you in the eye, not over your shoulder. They are other-focused; caring, not complaining. Sometimes such people undergo great suffering, yet after being with them you feel they have built you up. You intended to help them, but in fact you were the beneficiary!

These are individuals. But is there a whole family, a whole church that is like this? We all have our weak points, but nonetheless my answer is that there are many. In fact, I believe that in my own town there are dozens. I am glad to be living in my city at such a time as this.

I believe that those who care for the poor and the poor in spirit are a joy. It was among the down and outs in Paris that I fell in love, as it were, with the poor. Previously I had not lived anywhere near them, but there I found them on my doorstep, and I loved them and became, in my own small way, a part of them. I now believe it to be a self-evident truth that the Church must lean towards providing love and justice to the poor and disadvantaged. A community without the disabled among it will be a disabled community. A church without the marginalised in it is a marginalised church. I like it when there are dogs in church. Not because I like blessing pets, but because they are often a sign that the addicted and the poor are present. I learnt this in inner-city Paris, where we hosted a homeless people's breakfast on two mornings a week. This was quite simply a privilege.

Jesus said that we meet him and minister to him when we serve among the poor. It was Jackie Pullinger in Hong Kong who pointed out to me that to 'serve the poor' is patronising. Whereas to 'serve among the poor' allows you to admit that you are one of them. As we learn this and work in this way, what happens is that there is a connection with Christ and with his heart that is edifying to and replenishes our souls.

Following the season of personal healing I went through in

Paris, our Sunday service in Belleville was quite frequently interrupted by a bearded Zairian refugee who would shout out '*Je t'aime Papa, je t'aime!*' ('I love you, Daddy, I love you!') as he lurched drunkenly up the aisle before being steered back out to a corridor, if we could so persuade him. We called him Le Professeur Zaza because he insisted that was his name. His brain had lost some capacity during some terrible African war through intense suffering and the loss of all those dear to him. But we loved him. And when I visited his deathbed in hospital and experienced his strong love and gratitude, I reflected on the paradoxical combination of joy and delight at doing God's will, mingled with the suffering we share in as we touch the lives of broken people.

Jesus said we will meet him in the poor. This is a mystery, but one which any person involved in such works of love will understand. There is truth in his words: 'whatever you did for one of the least of these brothers of mine, you did for me.'[1] This then is the privilege of love. As Mother Teresa puts it: 'We are really contemplatives in the heart of the world. For we are touching the Body of Christ twenty-four hours.' It is this idea of touching that we need to get hold of.

I recently left for work from my home in the heart of my city and was confronted by the sight of a crowd of homeless people warming themselves from the hot air blowing out of the heating vents of the fitness centre opposite my house. Their presence reminded me how much more there is to do if we are truly to be the Church in our city. But as I chatted with them, one asked, 'Which church are you the pastor of?' I told them and then heard them say this: 'Ah, that's a Love church.' 'What do you mean?' I asked. 'Well, they love people in there: that's an Alpha church, isn't it?' This conversation warmed my heart. Behind it was the recognition that something meaningful was expressed through the weekly meals offered at the Alpha course, which offers conversation about Christianity to anyone interested; through the discipleship groups for marginalised people; and through the community meal we offer to all on Sundays. In these and in our mentoring and restoration programmes, love is being poured out over our city-centre residents. We are imperfect vessels – but what a privilege to hear that these efforts are noted. May we grasp this – and get involved in it.

It is interesting to note that the whole of Mother Teresa's ministry to the poor was born out of a vision of Christ on the cross saying, 'I thirst.' This was an epiphany that changed her life forever. It happened on a train from Calcutta to Darjeeling, as she was en route to her annual retreat. This is how she would explain this to her sisters:

'I thirst', Jesus said on the cross when He was deprived of every consolation, dying in absolute poverty, left alone, despised and broken in body and soul. He spoke of His thirst, not for water – but for love, for sacrifice. Jesus is God: therefore His love, His thirst is infinite. Our aim is to quench this infinite thirst of a God made man. Just like the adoring angels in heaven ceaselessly sing the praises of God, so the Sisters, using the four vows of Absolute Poverty, Chastity, Obedience and Charity towards the poor ceaselessly quench the thirsting God by their love and the love of souls they bring to Him.[2]

We see that Teresa understood this thirst of Christ's to be not for water but for love. From this vision there came into being a community that has inspired thousands, and won the Nobel Peace Prize. Its mission statement says: 'The General

End of the missionaries of Charity is to satiate the thirst of Jesus Christ on the Cross for love and Souls.'[3]

All over the world there are churches filled with world-changing joy-bringers. They are the unsung Mother Teresas of the planet and they have been the mainstay of God's kingdom throughout the history of the Church, from ancient times to the present. Wherever and whenever people have been filled with the Spirit of God, been healed, caught the 'little foxes' that ruin the vineyard, obeyed the Word of God and felt the heart of God, there has been epiphany and there has been a display of the true Church: the gracious and glorious bride of Christ.

I believe that one consequence of the Church submitting to the easy yoke of Christ's healing has been to give birth to what might be called a 'history of love' which, though often hidden, shows the continuity of God's actions through his followers down the ages.

Throughout the medieval period the Church always took a percentage of tithes to give to hospitality for the traveller and medication for the poor. The first ever sanctuary for battered wives was at Fontevaud Abbey in the twelfth century. Despite some tragic episodes along the way, the Church has brought life to the world. Education, medication and provisions have always been given by the Church. The first hospice for the dying was a Christian one. Journalist Malcolm Muggeridge, a former Communist, was converted through witnessing the ministry of Mother Teresa pouring out her life for the poorest of the poor in Calcutta – despite opposition from Hindu scholars, rebuking her for interfering with karma. Muggeridge noted: 'I have never come across an orphanage run by the Fabian or humanist society.'[4]

Many things spring to mind as examples of such love

expressed in action: organisations such as Tear Fund, the Red Cross, Christian Aid, World Vision, The Leprosy Mission, Amnesty International, Soul in the City, Betel, Arocha, Viva Network, International Justice Mission. The spirit of justice led Christians to pioneer the Socialist movement, the Feminist movement, the Peace movement, the Abolition of Slavery movement, the Temperance movement. Wherever the love of God is invited, there a passion for justice is ignited. If we just glance through a small window into the Church's great hall of fame of those filled with God's spirit of justice, we see St Francis loving creation and pouring out his life for the poor; William Wilberforce shattering the chains of slavery; Shaftesbury passing laws to protect children at work; Dr Barnardo loving the fatherless and giving the orphan a home; William Booth wresting prostitutes and alcoholics from the shadows; Hannah Moore seeking to educate the poor; Jackie Pullinger in Hong Kong building hostel-homes for addicts young and old, and lovingly seeing them through a 'cold turkey' night of deliverance with ceaseless loving prayer; Heidi Baker loving and feeding the poorest of the planet in Mozambique. This is just a small handful of the people sacrificing their lives for others amidst the cesspits of society.

Usually, these movements have been brought to birth through some kind of personal revelation of the love of God – an epiphany, if you like. The founding father or mother has been quite simply arrested by the love of God and has been unable to rest without passing it on. Or, more precisely, they have found their rest in giving that love away.

The apostle John said: 'We love because he first loved us.' As we allow his eyes of love to gaze into our past and catch the mischievous foxes in order to set us free, we will find we have a love to give away that is authentic and full of power. Churches are emerging across the globe where you can truly 'feel the love'; churches that are a joy to their city.

I want to be part of that.

Cranmer's Collect for 'the Sunday called Quinquagessima'[5]
O Lord, who dost teach us that our doings without charity are nothing worth, send thy Holy Ghost and pour into our hearts that most excellent gift of charity, the very bond of peace and all virtues, without the which whosoever liveth is counted dead before thee; grant this for thy only Son Jesus Christ's sake. Amen.

The most critical need of the Church at this moment is men – the right kind of men, bold men. The talk is that we need revival, that we need a new baptism of the Holy Spirit – and God knows we must have both – but God will not revive mice. He will not fill rabbits with the Holy Spirit.

We languish for men who feel themselves expendable in the warfare of the soul because they have already died to the allurements of this world. Such men will be free from the compulsions that control weaker men. They will not be forced to do things by the squeeze of circumstances. Their only compulsion will come from within – or from above. This kind of freedom is necessary if we are to have prophets in our pulpits again instead of mascots.

A.W. Tozer, *This World: Playground or Battleground?*

To give, and not to count the cost
to fight, and not to heed the wounds,
to toil, and not to seek for rest,
to labour, and not to ask for any reward,
save that of knowing that we do thy will.
St Ignatius of Loyola

CHAPTER FOURTEEN

Self-Denying

No meditation on epiphany and love is complete without a serious consideration of Jesus' statement: 'Greater love has no one than this, that he lay down his life for his friends.'[1] In Jesus' definition of love, self-sacrifice on behalf of others is the greatest love of all. Saints who have done this in the past have often testified to 'seeing heaven open'.

Jesus does not scatter the attribute adjective 'great' about liberally. But one place where he does use it is in his description of his cousin John. Of him he says: 'Among those born of women there has not risen anyone greater than John the Baptist.'[2] Such was the verdict of the ultimate judge of character. Of course, the angel prophesied before his birth: 'He will be great in the sight of the Lord.'[3]

John the Baptist was great – and he laid down his life on behalf of humankind. He had challenged Herod to the core of his being. Herod had him arrested, 'yet he liked to listen to him'.[4] John was great in sacrifice, great in his passion for justice and great in the sight of the Lord. I would say John was filled with a 'greater love'.

Those who give up their lives have most deeply understood how to live and move 'in the sight of the Lord'. For there are many who seek to be great in the sight of men. We can be tempted to seek the limelight, we can develop what has been called 'approval addiction', we may yearn to succeed in the eyes of our peers. It seems only relatively few have cut free simply to seek or enter into greatness in the eyes of God. Yet in history this self-sacrifice has been the distinctive mark of the Church. Such noble desire has often got buried under the rubble of time, resurgent ambition and collective amnesia. But through stories of the Church's loving martyrs, this true greatness shines through. Theirs is a history of courage, sacrifice, self-forgetfulness and love, and I thank God we are seeing just such a commitment come back today. I will seek to inspire this 'greater love' as we walk through history, gazing at a cloud of witnesses, that we, in the end, might be like them.

Before we set off, I must warn you that this path to 'downward mobility' will come close to killing us. But I guess that is the point.

When I felt God was calling my family to move to inner-city Paris, to my flesh it seemed like a move of death because of the downward mobility it promised to bring. Paris may sound 'cool' in theory, but the poverty-stricken area of Belleville that we were heading to is dirty, deprived, multicultural and near-impossible for the Church. Or so it seemed to me the first time I went there, despite feeling the call of God. I would take a 50 per cent cut in salary, housing, security, 'visibility'; schooling for the children would be compromised. Influence on the wider body of Christ would go. We would, I felt, 'disappear'.

I remember sleepless nights when I wrestled with the 'impossibility' of God asking me to do such a thing. I felt my children would (metaphorically) die there – such was my sin, stupidity and short-sightedness. It was not enough to cling in my sleep-deprived state to scriptures about leaving houses and inheriting eternal life. In short, I discovered I was a pathetic coward! I discovered how tenacious were my expectations that, as life went on, I would better my living conditions – go upwards, get richer and 'live bigger' – ideas utterly foreign to Christ's teaching. I justified them because of my family – 'it would not be fair on my children for them to suffer' (by which I meant that they might not have the same materialistic excess as their contemporaries). I little realised how much we suffer if, in fact, we have too much. How much we suffer if we never 'learn to lean'. In the end we did go down this path, moved out of our comfortable denomination and church setup, and all our worldly security. And it was gloriously, unspeakably joyful to have to lean on God for everything for a season. We learnt things that God simply could not have taught us without these testing circumstances. Now, back in my own country, I try not to forget them.

What took us there was not any truly great love; it was just one small step of sacrifice for the sake of loving French people! But when we come to the real thing, the list of men and women of great love in the sight of God is long and challenging. Moses left the treasures of Egypt, breaking with their hold out in the wilderness through a revelation on holy ground, loving his people so much that he broke them out of slavery. There was Elijah, 'a man just like us', who was prepared to live with nothing to learn dependence on God for the love of his people. He prayed to God and witnessed a dramatic intervention – fire from heaven and an end to drought – which brought and signalled deliverance from the grip of Baal and idolatry.[5]

Then there was Daniel, who risked his life and would not stop praying even though it was against the law, and was saved from lions. Later he saw heaven opened and prophesied of 'one like a son of man', the 'Ancient of Days' – in words so great they echo down the ages. Daniel's friends in the furnace had the same love for God upon them, to the extent that they were prepared to lay down their lives as witnesses for humanity, saying in words that every Christian should memorise as a life motto: 'If we are thrown into the blazing furnace, the God we serve is able to save us from it, and he will rescue us from your hand, O king. But even if he does not, we want you to know, O king, that we will not serve your gods or worship the image of gold you have set up.'[6]

Much later Stephen, a simple helper at tables but one who would not stop talking of the one in heaven, got himself arrested and became the first Christian martyr (the second if you include John the Baptist), but not before he too had had his epiphany – he saw heaven opened and the Lord Jesus at the right hand of God.[7] All of these we can agree had this 'greater love' and were 'great in the sight of the Lord'. But I believe that we are called to be so too.

Leaping over fifteen centuries of history, we see another martyr, this time in Oxford, thrusting his 'unworthy right hand' into the raging flames, telling the crowd 'as long as the flames would let him: I see heaven open and Jesus at the right hand of God'.[8] Such epiphanies often accompany such sacrifice.

For us in the twenty-first century after Christ, we know there are Christians who have wrestled with what it means to have this greater love and to be great in the sight of God – to love God and love people. Often this choice leads them (and could lead us) into conflict with the powers that be in this world. One of the issues for us to settle is this: are we prepared to suffer and be in conflict with the powers of this world if God so calls?

When Dietrich Bonhoeffer was first arrested in 1944, he

had wrestled with and resolved this question already: 'The Cross is not the end to an otherwise god-fearing and happy life, but it meets us at the beginning of our communion with Christ. When Christ calls a man, he bids him come and die.'[9] He left a glittering academic career in America for the sake of identification with his fellow Germans. Like Paul before him, he chose prison instead of power; self-sacrifice instead of safety. He objected to the regime that he called the antichrist, Hitler's Nazi party. In prison that first month he puzzled about greatness, drawn to the story of Baruch. 'I keep coming back to Jeremiah 45:5,' he said. 'Should you then seek great things for yourself? Seek them not.'[10] This prince of a man, this giant among Germans, was certainly great in the sight of the Lord – and paid the ultimate price. As he was led to his death by firing squad a week before the surrender of Germany, his last words were: 'This is the end – for me the beginning of life.' On that day, his life in heaven began; and also his lively influence on earth, and he still speaks to us boldly through his insightful and challenging books on ethics and community, which he describes as 'life together', as well as the 'cost of discipleship', which he described so brilliantly and then demonstrated so clearly with the loss of his life.

There are perhaps two great questions to resolve in life. Bonhoeffer had settled both of them. The first is: Will I live a life of love? Then, secondly: Will I give up my life for love? Apparently it is possible to love without greatness. But at the same time, it is possible to be a martyr without love, in which case it means nothing. Paul writes: 'If I give all I possess to the poor and surrender my body to the flames, but have not love, I gain nothing.'[11] Martyrdom without love is not enough. Sacrifice without love for God and for people is not a glory, but is worthless.[12] And on the other hand, if we say we love without any willingness to give up our lives, we remain weak: a poor shadow of greater love. Paul writing of love in marriage says a husband needs to love his wife and give himself up for her 'as Christ loved the church and gave himself up for her'.[13] This evidently does not mean one immediately steps in front of a firing squad for one's wife's sake. It begins with a daily breaking down of our own selfishness and making joyful choices to die to self and live for the other that, paradoxically, are what will make marriage a joy and a delight.

Perhaps the epiphany needed for a loving marriage, or any major endeavour that involves us committing ourselves in relationship, is simply a true sight of Christ's sacrifice, which calls and enables us to live the same way.

Another question we have to answer is whether we are willing to give up the quest for greatness in the sight of the world. For if we forget going after greatness in the sight of the world but instead follow God; if we lovingly become the 'least', then we have begun the road to true greatness and greater love. And that godly greatness is so sorely needed today in every sphere of life: from politics to preaching, from policing to prison visiting, from social work to sports, from teaching to personal training. Wherever we may find ourselves, I believe we need a completely new kind of loving leadership: leadership that gives more than it receives.

The desire to achieve greatness in the sight of men is hard to shake off, but is settled when we are willing to decide to give up our life. I fear that worldly ambition is one of the single most powerful idolatries in the very place it should be banned: the Church. Instead of being a house of prayer for all nations, she becomes a marketplace of competing programmes and activities! Even those closest to Christ can apparently be pushed off track by their ambition. It may not even be to do with immediate gratification but a reaching out towards our status in the afterlife: the close disciples James and John both asked for a seat next to Christ in heaven and were told it was, 'Not so with you. Instead, whoever wants to become great among you must be your servant.'[14]

A healthy ambition for a church and a life is this: just to be a loving servant. Paradoxically, those who have made this decision and stuck to it for his sake are often the ones that history remembers in the end. The danger for many of us is that in serving the Church we bring our human skills to bear and become servants of ourselves. We become focused on succeeding in the eyes of men, but I believe in so doing we lose touch with God. We have great ambitions or dreams which we see as honouring God. But considering what is famous or lauded in the Church in the West, sometimes I shake my head and wonder. Stories of high-profile leaders who 'crash and burn' remind us how vulnerable the very best can be. The Church is before the watching world, and the Church that will make a difference will not be one that is advancing her empire, but one that has broken with addictions and ambition. Instead she has her heart truly set on being great for the sake of heaven; not famous on earth, perhaps not in the slightest bit outwardly successful on earth.

If we get hold of this it can lead to a great liberation and freedom. It can be such a blessed relief for church leaders to know they can be free from this. Many of us get caught on the 'fork' of ambition, speared on the prongs of career, lifestyle, possessions. But Christ comes and bends that fork into a cross: calls us simply to love him and to love people; a calling that is simple but deep, and a great liberation. He calls us downwards, to meet the needs of the needy, even to face death if necessary – as he has called saints before, those who have made a difference.

The numbers of those who have done this are countless, but they are all special. One such was Haik Hovsepian from Iran. Haik began ministry as a pastor and eventually served as president of the Assemblies of God churches in his country. His story is told, among other places, on the DVD 'Cry From Iran'.[15] Every account of him testifies of a gentle, godly servant to all he met. He tirelessly protected and defended those oppressed and suffering, visiting widows and orphans in the time of great sadness and persecution that has come upon Christians in that land. As I watched him recently on film, I loved him. Among many deeds of mercy – too many to number – he publicised one pastor's case before the world's press and parliaments and, with documentary evidence of illegal imprisonment and the international outcry that followed sentencing from the Teheran regime, secured that pastor's release. But after this, he himself was 'taken where he did not want to go', shot several times and buried in an unmarked grave (discovered later through a brave gravedigger's tip-off). A martyr, he disappeared from the face of the earth. But I dare say he was great in the sight of God.

Can whole communities become great in the sight of God? They can and must. It is possible, and we are seeing it. It happens in a sense unwillingly, for who can 'will' suffering upon themselves? But in the Church in India, in China, in Indonesia, in Nigeria, in Pakistan, in Afghanistan, in Egypt, we may come upon true greatness. I found it recently in the tear-stained faces of those in the suffering, hidden, often dispossessed Church in China. I've just completed a journey to China and met some of these people. One is a pastor in a certain important city,[16] imprisoned from time to time, but currently building a church at the back of a bus park, and serving a network of thousands, travelling to several suburbs – having just managed to buy a moped to replace his trusty bicycle. When I asked him to describe his church he said: 'We want just to be known for our love.' He and his wife then described to me how they are serving food and providing 'soaking prayer' to cancer sufferers in a hidden hangar (where indeed his wife often sleeps at night) to help relieve the suffering of a hundred people in a kind of healing hospice. Surely this is 'greater love'?

Another Chinese pastor turned down lucrative job offers in America after winning a starred PhD there, giving up safety to return to his home country and life in the underground church. He is building a training centre in the suburbs of another large city for sixty students and a church of 1,500, invisible to those in authority but visible and fruitful in the eyes of heaven.

Even of course in the peaceful West, many are the similar stories of 'greater love' and sacrifice. Hospice care and drug addiction relief is not just to be found in China.[17] The question we must ask is: Am I, are my family and my community, part of this?

It is not surprising that sometimes this opportunity to suffer and serve comes on by chance, such as in a time of war. In times of suffering and attack people often discover greatness within them in a way that is unusual in quieter times. During the fighting of the First World War, stories of extraordinary courage came to light. For example, in Oxford the name of Chavasse is revered – Noel Chavasse was the most decorated soldier of the war, winning the Military Cross and then, twice, the Victoria Cross. He was the twin brother of

C.M. Chavasse, Rector of St Aldates, where I serve, later Bishop of Rochester and then the first Master of St Peter's College, Oxford.

Noel Chavasse was first awarded the VC for his actions on 9 August 1916, at Guillemont, France. He looked after the wounded all that day under heavy fire and, during the night, he continued searching for the wounded in front of the enemy's lines. Next day, under heavy shell fire, he and a stretcher-bearer carried an urgent case 500 yards to safety, although he was wounded himself during the journey. The same night, with twenty volunteers, he rescued three wounded men from a shell-hole only thirty-six yards from enemy trenches. Altogether he saved the lives of some twenty wounded men.

His second VC was earned in August 1917. Although severely wounded early in the action, while carrying a wounded officer to the dressing station, he refused to leave his post and went out repeatedly under heavy fire to attend the wounded. During this time, although without food, heavy with fatigue and faint from his wounds, he helped to carry in other badly wounded men, being instrumental in saving many who would otherwise have died in the bad weather. In the end he himself died of his wounds. Extraordinary, sacrificial, Christ-like love from a physician who gave up his life for others: let this be the mark of the community called the Church.

His father, the Bishop of Liverpool, wrote to another son, informing him of Noel's death:

You will have heard by this time that our dearest Noel has been called away . . . Our hearts are almost broken, for oh! How we loved him. Your dearest mother is pathetic in her grief, so brave and calm notwithstanding. But again and again, we keep praising and thanking God for having given us such a son. We know he is with Christ, and that one day – perhaps soon – we shall see him again. What should we do in such sorrow as this, if we could not rest on the character of God, on his love, and wisdom and righteousness?[18]

The war still went on. Early in September a letter from Lord Derby arrived at the Bishop's Palace that made the bishop break down in tears. It read:

I signed something last night which gave me the most mixed feelings of deep regret and great pleasure and that was that a Bar should be granted to the Victoria Cross gained by your son . . . While it cannot in any way diminish your sorrow, still from the point of view of those who are your friends, it is a great pleasure to think that your son in laying down his life laid it down on behalf of his fellow countrymen . . . In all the records of Victoria Crosses given I do not think there is one that will appeal to the British Public more than the record for which this Bar is to be given.

I think it good to revisit these memorials in our history, that we might 'un-forget' the jewel-like people who have preceded us. In the Second World War, Winston Churchill called forth the courage and greatness of a whole country with his evocative phrasings: 'Death and ruin have become small things compared with the shame of defeat in the field of duty'; 'Never in the field of human conflict was so much owed by so many to so few'[19]; 'I have nothing to offer but blood, toil, tears and sweat'. Churchill's greatness came from vision and courage: the capacity to paint the big picture and to call forth sacrifice. The following words show his extraordinary leadership when he painted a word picture of the world's prospects after the evacuation of Dunkirk:

> The Battle for France is over. I expect that the Battle of Britain is about to begin. Upon this battle depends the survival of Christian civilisation . . . Hitler knows that he will have to break us in this Island or lose the war. If we can stand up to him, all Europe may be free . . . But if we fail, then the whole world, including the United States, including all we have known and cared for, will sink into the abyss of a new Dark Age made more sinister, and perhaps more protracted, by the lights of perverted science. Let us therefore brace ourselves for our duties, and so bear ourselves that if the British . . . Commonwealth last for a thousand years, men will still say, 'This was their finest hour.'[20]

It is this sense of love, sacrifice and destiny, applied for the sake of God's kingdom, that qualifies us for the possibility of being 'great in the sight of the Lord'.

We should speak, too, of communities in India, in Indonesia, in Iran and in Pakistan and China that are exhibiting the true greatness that God desires. Extreme stories of sacrificial, non-violent courage which pours out love abound in those places: they are the mark of the Church's true greatness.

Let us turn to those working for justice. Martin Luther King Jr had this quality of greatness. His dream was clear and compelling: 'I have a dream that one day this nation will rise up and live out the true meaning of its creed: "We hold these truths to be self-evident that all men are created equal" . . . I have a dream that my four little children will one day live in a nation where they will not be judged by the colour of their skin but by the content of their character. I have a dream today.'[21]

On the eve of his assassination, he reflected on the danger he might be in, but put his vision for justice ahead of any thoughts of himself. In an eerie parallel of Moses' final encounter with God, looking out over the Promised Land, he spoke thus:

> Well, I don't know what will happen now. We've got some difficult days ahead. But it doesn't matter with me now. Because I've been to the mountain-top and I don't mind . . . I may not get there with you. But I want you to know tonight that we, as a people, will get to the Promised Land. And I'm happy tonight. I'm not worried about anything. I'm not fearing any man. Mine eyes have seen the glory of the coming of the Lord.[22]

The next evening he was on a hotel balcony when he was hit by an assassin's bullet, and died. It was 4 April 1968. Fifty years later, the election of Barak Obama as the first African American president of the United States brought evidence of the extent to which King's dream has been achieved.

Nelson Mandela is another in the same movement to break the chains of racism. He was not afraid, I believe for the sake of love, to pay with his life. His words at the trial that put him into prison on Robben Island for twenty-seven long years continue to move me whenever I read them:

> During my lifetime I have dedicated myself to this struggle of the African people. I have fought against white domination, and I have fought against black domination. I have

cherished the ideal of a democratic and free society in which all persons live together in harmony with equal opportunities. It is an ideal which I hope to live for and to see realised. But if needs be, it is an ideal for which I am prepared to die.[23]

Mandela eventually emerged from the desert of his imprisonment and enforced silence to go from prison to presidency in a Joseph-like move that saved his land from a bloodbath. It is a measure of his greatness to see the respectful esteem in which Mandela is held by those of every colour and background throughout South Africa today, but it would not have happened without his expression of that 'greater love', of being prepared to lay down his life for his people.

Christians who go down to meet with the poorest of the poor are likewise 'great in the sight of the Lord'. Mother Teresa's entire motivation sprang from the twin commitments to love and abandonment of self-interest that this chapter has sought to demonstrate are the keys to truly showing love. Accepting the Nobel Peace Prize she said: 'There is so much suffering, so much hatred, so much misery and we, with our prayer, with our sacrifice are beginning at home. Love begins at home, and it is not how much we do but how much love we put into the action that we do. And with this prize that I have received as a prize for peace I am going to try to make a home for the many people who have no home . . . '[24]

For those of us not living in a war zone, this helps us to see where and how we begin to live a life of 'greater love'. It begins at home as we make a choice and put it into action. It may involve 'downward mobility', but I believe it absolutely begins with twofold decision. First to take the path of love daily, and second, the measured decision to give up our life. I don't know which is more challenging. Both are demanding in different ways. But drawing inspiration from the stories above, let us resolve to believe firmly that both are possible, for us as much as for these heroes of faith and commitment.

Collect for Self-Denying

Lord Jesus, you showed us greater love when you laid down your life for your friends. Mercifully grant that we might be given grace to follow that great cloud of witnesses who have done the same, that through the gift of courage and love our land may again know you. We ask this in Jesus' name. Amen.

The response to war is to live like brothers and sisters.
The response to injustice is to share. The response to
despair is a limitless trust and hope. The response to
prejudice and hatred is forgiveness. To work for
community is to work for humanity . . . it is to work
for the Kingdom of God. It is to work to enable every
one to live and taste the secret joys of the human
person united to the eternal.
Jean Vanier, *Community and Growth*

I am looking for my brothers.
Genesis 37:16

CHAPTER FIFTEEN

Searching

'I am looking for my brothers.' This evocative sentence is found in the story of Joseph. I introduce it because I think it will be part of a lover's lifestyle to be searching for his brothers, her sisters. Joseph is an 'epiphany man'. He dreams of the future influence God is calling him to. He blurts it out to his family, and they take offence. When he is sent by his father out into the fields a man finds him and asks him what he is doing and he gives the reply: 'I am looking for my brothers.' At first glance this is an entirely ordinary exchange: a boy is engaged in doing what his father has asked him and is looking for his brothers. He meets a man – who is, perhaps, an angel? Joseph's answer is apparently straightforward, but I think it can be an epiphany phrase to sum up a life, maybe our own life. I am looking for my brothers in my family, my church, my city, my nation, my continent.

When the Son of God stepped into life on earth, arguably he too was looking for his brothers. He came to reconcile. Joseph is a forerunner of the one before whom all the twelve tribes will bow down, who is looking and searching for his brothers.

I have had a couple of epiphanies as far as working for unity is concerned. I remember the first time I 'saw' this call on my life: it was listening to a talk on 'trinity unity' from John 17. The speaker was reflecting on Jesus' prayer 'that they may be one as we are one': what Jesus calls us to is the highest level of confidence, submission, trust and respect, as seen in the relationship between Father, Son and Holy Spirit. I remember thinking: this is something to aspire to – a unity between a town's churches where competition or rivalry is unheard of, where each one is complementing the other's work, just as in the Trinity. If Jesus prayed for this, we should believe it is possible. I remember thinking: this is something to devote one's life to.

Love will be looking for reconciled relationships, for reunions. Just as it should within our physical family, it can also apply to our spiritual family. I remember that, when I was called to go and serve in the city of Oxford, Nicky Gumbel, founder of the Alpha course and now vicar of Holy Trinity Brompton, asked what I felt some of my priorities might be. I replied that I felt called to help bring the 'twelve tribes' of evangelicalism in Oxford together. While our city has borne a lot of fruit and many owe their spiritual birth to experiences of the presence of God in Oxford, a sad side has been long histories of rivalry between charismatic and evangelical camps in Oxford, particularly among students. These disagreements were a common thread for generations of Oxford people, it seemed. Nicky listened and then said: 'But Charlie, isn't it time to bring the twelve tribes of Christianity together? Isn't that more interesting?' My response to this is: ultimately, yes; but timing is everything!

At a time of deep internal contestation, on the night he was betrayed, Jesus prayed his last considered prayer. The burden of his energy was to make one repeated request of his Father: that his disciples might be one, so that the world may believe. That is why I am looking for my brothers.

In Genesis 37, Joseph is looking for his brothers. They aren't looking for him. But he accepts the challenge to 'go and bring a report'. His brothers do not receive him well. They see him coming and decide to kill him, though then change their minds and sell him for twenty pieces of silver. Years later, the Bible records how David, another younger brother, is told by his father Jesse to look for his brothers: 'See how your brothers are and bring back some assurances from them.'[1] It is a strikingly similar request – with a sadly similar response from said brothers. Eliab, David's oldest brother, reacts thus: 'Why have you come down here? . . . I know how conceited you are and how wicked your heart is.'[2]

Note the way these brothers permit themselves to be so hateful to each other. Sadly, this occurs all too often today, even in the Church. But I am still looking for my brothers. I believe there is a prophetic mantle on those looking for unity. In this story, David is perceived as a conceited pain by his brothers with his righteous indignation about Goliath's taunts. He is a young upstart, a dreamer just like Joseph. But, just like Joseph, he is the one on whom God's hand rests and will, even though young, defeat Goliath!

Joseph was sent to look for his brothers. David was sent to seek out his brothers. Then, in the fullness of time, at last, Jesus came looking for his brothers. Sent by the Father of all, he has been looking out across the ages, longing to bring all scattered things back together under one head. Jesus came to seek and save that which was lost. He came to his own. And his own received him not. He was despised and rejected, he came from light as the light into darkness – thick darkness. And he was hated for it. He came to reconcile. And I want to say that a lover of God will be the same. That person – perhaps you – will be dreaming; dreaming of being the Church in the midst of your city, your community, for the sake of our civilisation.

I am looking for my brothers – in my family, church, city, nation, world. And I am paradoxically encouraged that Jesus' brothers didn't believe in him. They said to him: 'Since you are doing these things, show yourself to the world.' Then it goes on, 'For even his own brothers did not believe in him.'[3] In time, of course, Jesus' brother James became the leader of the church in Jerusalem and his young brother Jude touchingly wrote of his older brother as the one 'who is able to keep us from falling'.[4] Jesus found and was recognised by his brothers.

As for Joseph, he too eventually created community. Where his brothers wanted to kill him, God deflected their aim to keep him safe. Where they betrayed, God was true to his promise and to the dream he had given. What they meant for harm, God meant for good. Joseph had a dream – and he went looking for his brothers.

Like so many, it was when he was young that he had this dream. Perhaps because he was the youngest, his brothers were jealous and envious. Murderously so. This is a common theme in the Bible, and indeed in life – someone has a dream, or a calling given from God, but they are hated and rejected for it. In the end, in one of the most moving reconciliation scenes ever written, surely a preview of heaven in the same way that Joseph prefigures Christ, Joseph finds his brothers and his father again. Everyone is crying. Joseph can hardly believe the immensity of the reversal. All his people come down to join him. There is reconciliation; there is restoration; there is rest and – what is more for them all – the long years of famine are over.

Joseph was looking for his physical brothers. They had scorned him and they hated him, but he was still looking for them. In beginning to apply this, I believe our first responsibility is to love our close family, our literal brothers and sisters. The person drawn by love will be drawn to connecting with his brothers. Yet in our broken world, so many families struggle to find each other and to have fellowship.

In the view of Douglas Coupland, who wrote *Generation X: Tales for an Accelerated Culture* and for whom the term 'post-christian Christian' was invented, 'All families are psychotic. Everybody has basically the same family – it's just reconfigured slightly different from one to the next.'[5] He puts it ironically, but if we stop to think, it is a phrase that has a ring of truth. If you look at the stories of Cain and Abel, Jacob and Esau, Joseph and his brothers, the children of King David – the Absalom generation – it is certainly true of several prominent families in the Bible.

Let us ponder for a moment the chaotic intrigue in King David's family. There is already jealousy in the previous generation, from David's brothers as he arrives with the dream of killing Goliath. After he becomes king, there is weakness in the life of David when he fails to deal with his daughter's rape or his son Absalom's revenge. He half-reconciles with Absalom, but it is this that in the end leads to further chaos, betrayal, civil war and death. Further weakness is evident in his adultery with Bathsheba, a sexual weakness apparently transmitted to his son Solomon, whose multiple marriages and subsequent spiritual adultery lead in the next generation to the demise of the kingdom. There is a catalogue of emotional unhealthiness and chaos infecting his family tree.

Yet this is common today. In his novel *Life After God*, Coupland tells this haunting story about the narrator's sister:

Over the next few years, Laurie began systematically to go through all of the family members and her friends, finding some small slight the person had committed, whether real or imagined, then magnifying that slight out of all proportion, then cutting that person off forever. It wasn't too long before everyone had been axed, my mother being the last to go.

And it was shortly after this that she simply . . . faded away. To Seattle? To Phoenix? To Toronto? No big farewell scene. Nothing definitive. Just a fading away five years ago. And since then, she has been like the family undead person, never alluded to – erased as though she never existed.

But families can't just forget one of their own. Despite the failure of their attempts to track her down, Coupland goes on:

Yet of course her presence is felt – at family dinners and weddings and so forth. But it is especially felt at Christmas morning when her presence floats around the yard outside the windows, mocking, fleeting, above the lawn and inside the forest, little glints and rustles which we know are her but which we dare not mention.[6]

This loss and separation happens increasingly often today. The Internet and mobile phone and social network connections have, paradoxically, made us the most disconnected people in the history of the world. And I believe we are often most in danger of losing connection with our brothers, sisters, mothers, fathers and children.

For myself, I come from a family where my father, uncle and aunt all got divorced, and my siblings number eleven in total (two brothers, two sisters, two half-sisters, one half-brother, two step-brothers and two step-sisters), of whom nine have spouses or partners, making a total of twenty people. And this is to say nothing of the dozens of children and grandchildren. With numbers like this, dysfunction is never far round the corner! In fact, miraculously, I belong to a family where, largely thanks to my amazing mother, all these siblings get on well and love each other and enjoy the time they spend with each other. There has been no breakdown in affection; there have been no situations where people refuse to talk to each other – thank God. But it is complex and has sometimes been strained. Even for 'nuclear' families with no divorces, and including 'Christian families', I observe that it is not necessarily easier. Often, because of high expectations, there is even greater disappointment, then painful fallout and even, tragically, complete relationship breakdown. This is why, when preparing people for marriage, and wedding plans get hairy, I cheerfully say, 'All families are potentially a little bit psychotic: don't despair!'

We live in a collapsing culture where families are under extreme pressure. In T.S. Eliot's play 'The Family Reunion', the host describes her life's priority: 'I keep Wishwood alive to keep the family alive, to keep them together, to keep me alive, and I keep them.' Behind this we recognise an obsessiveness that can creep into families; but it is a creeping terror to be avoided. We need to reinvent our traditions.

One idea that can help is consciously reinventing family reunions. I am not talking about strained gatherings that are sources of stress. The key is to lower the expectations, to be thoughtful and forgiving; and to ask for forgiveness if needs be! I do believe it is worth taking – even creating – opportunities for family meals, parties, reunions, celebrations, anniversaries. Living in France for ten years, I learnt how to linger at meal times. Even Conseil Presbyteral (church council) meetings in that beloved country were helped to run smoothly by good food and excellent wine, but this should not surprise, for Jesus probably never presided over a business meeting and presumably intended his Church to be managed over meals and friendships. What a contrast to the twenty-four chairs around a boardroom table that greeted me on arrival at my first church council meeting in Oxford.

As we recover these intentional times together, there can be the opportunity to restore and deepen relationships. Reconciliation may need to occur among brothers. Forgiveness may need to flow.

If you are estranged, one thing I find useful is specifically to pray for the miracle of 'God's eyesight'. God's eyes survey the whole picture, going back to the beginning of the offence and 'seeing' not a sister who has been rude to you, a brother who has been drinking again – but a brother whose child was worryingly ill again, a sister whose job was intolerable and who let fly with you because she trusted you not to reject her. God can and will give 'forgiving and loving'-tinted spectacles and clear eyesight. Hopefully he will give them to my brothers as well, so that they can look at me, not as someone who talks too much or has too-strong opinions or who worries all the time, but as a friend who is trying to love God and love people. God 'causes his sun to rise on the evil and the good',[7] says Jesus. He is indiscriminate in his affection, whatever people have done, and so should we be.

Sometimes it is not reconciliation that is needed but the warming up of a love that has gone cold with neglect. Love has not turned bitter, but it is lukewarm. In that case, pray. Pray the collect below. Do the obvious: be in touch at birthdays, over Christmas. Go out of your way to connect. Then pray and ask God what to do and when he tells you, do it. To appropriate Christ's warning to the Ephesian church: remember the height you have fallen from; repent; and re-do the things that make for community in the family.[8] When this happens, look forward to deep joy. For, as the psalm says, 'How good and pleasant it will be when brothers dwell together in unity . . . It is as if the dew of Hermon were falling on Mount Zion. For there the LORD bestows his blessing, even life for evermore.'[9]

Widening our search from physical to spiritual brothers, we are in good company: that of Christ. He did of course care for his mother at the cross, loving her and providing for her. But earlier, he famously pronounced: '"Who is my mother, and who are my brothers?" Pointing to his disciples, he said, "Here are my mother and my brothers. For whoever does the will of my Father in heaven is my brother and sister and mother."'[10] It is clear that Jesus redefined family. And we must do so too, while at the same time caring deeply and dearly for our own flesh and blood.

As far as the Church is concerned, I'm not a Joseph – but I do have a dream. I hope I can communicate it. I'd like to see the body of Christ one in the earth, as the apostolic church was, walking and talking and arguing and living with Jesus. Love has opened my eyes to this dream, and love compels me to say that I want that unity. I believe that the 'Acts 2 Church' is a possibility. Not a lowest-common-denominator ecumenism, but a highest-common-factor unity of essential orthodoxy based on the apostolic doctrine of the cross. Not an English unity based on irony, but a heart unity as was found among the first believers. 'They devoted themselves to the apostles' teaching and to the fellowship, to the breaking of bread and to prayer . . . and the Lord added to their number daily those who were being saved.'[11] I long for this.

I learnt this in part from John Wimber, founder of the Vineyard churches, who was a father in God to so many. I remember him talking about an epiphany he had had, when he asked God which part of the Church he liked and he got the reply: 'I love it all.' 'What . . . really *all*?' 'Yes, all – even the snake-handling churches.' And he worked this out in practice. When I invited John to France in 1993, he said he would not come unless there were Catholics sharing the meeting with me. He said he had spoken at pastors' meetings where there were 3,000 pastors present – 'That's a lot of pastors,' he reminded me – but he said he would come to France for as few as six, provided Protestant and Catholic leaders were in the room and prepared to love each other and build together, 'because he loves the whole Church'. And some months later, true to his word, even though he was quite ill by then, he came. His visit was the trigger for future gatherings, *Embrase nos Coeurs*, which for a time gathered thousands who were likewise 'looking for their brothers'.

I have a great love for all Christians. I thank God that at last, in my city, new things are happening. There is unprecedented unity among so many Christian people through what we call the 'Love Oxford'[12] initiative. This was born some years ago, in this same spirit of 'searching for our brothers'. The public face of Love Oxford is an annual gathering on a Sunday morning of many churches, who all move their morning worship to this one open-air venue, so that we can not only be one in theory, but actually be in the same place, a few thousand of us together. It is a 'Family Reunion' – to use the title of Eliot's play. We meet to declare the praises of him who called us from darkness to light; pray for the peace of the city where God has placed us; and hear the distilled preaching of some of our city's pastors. This involves any and every denomination that wishes to be involved. It is for those who long for pan-Christian friendships. These gatherings have already born fruit, particularly among leaders who now choose to set aside time and prioritise friendships, via the happy experience of eating together frequently, and speaking truthfully and lovingly with each other. Love means that I am looking for my brothers. How about you? Have you had this unfolding epiphany?

Collect for Searching

O God, who sent your Son into our world to seek and to save that which was lost, mercifully grant that we being found by him may in turn look and seek and search for our brothers, not resting until we find them and are one in Jesus Christ our Lord. Amen.

We are asking the nations of Europe between whom
rivers of blood have flowed to forget the feuds of a
thousand years.
Winston Churchill, 'Ambition for Europe' broadcast,
14 February 1948

But he wanted to justify himself, so he asked Jesus,
'And who is my neighbour?'
Luke 10:29

CHAPTER SIXTEEN

Embracing: Overcoming prejudice

I lived for ten years in urban Essex, England. I once asked my neighbour where he was going for his holidays. He told me he would drive his caravan down to Spain, a country he loved visiting. 'Will you stop in France on the way?' I innocently asked. 'No, why would I do that? I hate the French,' was his unexpected reply. It was a conversation stopper, but caused me to think. Later, when I published a book in France, one of the endorsements spoke of '*les mille ans d'amour et de haine franco-anglais*' ('the thousand-year love/hate relationship between the French and the English'). One epiphany that God may give us is to challenge our prejudices. This happens for the apostle Peter through a truly remarkable 'zoo-ophany' (revelation of animals) dream recorded in Acts 10. It is bizarre but breathtaking.

> He saw heaven opened and something like a large sheet being let down to earth by its four corners. It contained all kinds of four-footed animals, as well as reptiles of the earth and birds of the air. Then a voice told him, 'Get up, Peter. Kill and eat.'
>
> 'Surely not, Lord!' Peter replied. 'I have never eaten anything impure or unclean.'
>
> The voice spoke to him a second time, 'Do not call anything impure that God has made clean.'

This happened three times, and immediately the sheet was taken back to heaven.

While Peter was wondering about the meaning of the vision, the men sent by Cornelius found out where Simon's house was and stopped at the gate. They called out, asking if Simon who was known as Peter was staying there. While Peter was still thinking about the vision, the Spirit said to him, 'Simon, three men are looking for you. So get up and go downstairs. Do not hesitate to go with them, for I have sent them.'[1]

Acts 10 goes on to detail the extraordinary conversion of Cornelius. But before Christ can convert Cornelius to himself, he must first convert Peter to Cornelius.

Peter is a Christian, an apostle, the head of the Church. But while his spirit has been made alive to God, it remains largely dead to the extent of God's plans for the world. True conversion lies in not only awakening to the Lord, but awakening to the lost. While we may be quick to convert to Christ, we can be reluctant to allow Christ to convert us to his will and way.

Peter was prejudiced against non-Jews. Culturally, his nation of Israel had been subjected to repeated invasions, occupations and persecutions by Gentile rulers including Persians, Greeks and Romans. This made Jewish people fearful of other peoples and inevitably insular. Moreover, theologically, Peter knew he was part of God's historic chosen people. The Jews' election and religion was predicated on distinction and enforced strict dietary laws, and hence social separation was necessary. A devout Jew could not share the food or the company of a Pagan or a Gentile and could not even enter their home.[2]

Peter's pride and prejudice was understandable, but his kosher lifestyle would keep him from the non-Jewish people whom Christ wanted to reach. The question we may need to consider carefully is: What will it take for us to overcome our prejudices and obey Christ? For Peter it would take three visions, three voices and three visitors. God brings Peter the startling revelation cited above. It is a vision of a sheet with four corners (representing the four corners of the world also seen in Revelation 7:1) and on it are animals of all kinds, including those defined as unclean by Jewish law. Three times this vision comes, three times the Lord says, 'Kill and eat.' Three times Peter refuses: 'I have never eaten anything impure or unclean.' Three times the Lord says: 'Do not call anything impure that God has made clean.'

In Jewish culture, repeating something three times indicated that whatever was said was given definitively and permanently. Christ universalised and intensified the moral law of the Old Testament. So 'don't murder' became 'don't get angry', and 'don't commit adultery' became 'don't lust'. But he annulled the Old Testament ceremonial law – questions of diet, days and rituals. Peter finds he must relinquish the ceremonial law if he is to fulfil his destiny. Along with the other disciples, Peter had received a mandate from Christ to go and make disciples of all nations. He had also received the great unction: Pentecost 'power to be witnesses'. Acts 8 tells us Peter was willing to evangelise in Judea, on his home turf, and even in Samaria (where there were half-Jews). But as yet, his racial prejudices had hampered his witness to the world beyond the Jewish community. Peter's prejudice militated against his obedience to the Great Commission.

In *Jane Eyre* Charlotte Brontë noted, 'Prejudices, it is well known, are most difficult to eradicate from the heart.'[3]

Prejudice can be a subtle thing, as we can see from Jane Austen's *Pride and Prejudice*: 'Elizabeth, having rather expected to affront him, was amazed at his gallantry . . . and Darcy had never been so bewitched by any woman as he was by her. He really believed, that were it not for the inferiority of her connections, he should be in some danger.'[4]

We are prejudiced when we think of ourselves as superior and another distinct group inferior, whether due to their race, creed, colour, age, class, gender, sexuality, shape, size, hair length, fashion, hair colour. In his autobiography, Mahatma Gandhi wrote how during his student days in London he read the Gospels and seriously considered converting to Christianity. He believed that in the teachings of Jesus he might find the solution to the caste system that was dividing the people of India. One Sunday, he attended a service at a nearby church, intending to talk to the minister about becoming a Christian. When he entered the sanctuary, however, the usher refused to give him a seat and suggested that he go worship with his own people. Gandhi left the church and never returned. 'If Christians have caste differences also,' he said, 'I might as well remain a Hindu.' That usher's racial prejudice, his failure to understand the global application of the gospel, betrayed Jesus and turned away a seeker who was to become of great significance.

Peter's revelation was needed because of his hesitation to obey the Great Commission as a result of prejudice. We need to ask: Against whom am I prejudiced? Perhaps it is homeless people, perhaps homeowners; perhaps whites, perhaps non-whites? Perhaps it is the poor? Or perhaps it is the rich? Perhaps Polish immigrants, or Pakistanis, or Muslims, or Catholics? Maybe the old, or the young? Maybe it is the French, the Chinese, Americans, the Jews?

Romans 2:11 insists: 'God does not show favouritism' and Galatians puts it this way in 3:28: 'There is neither Jew nor Greek, slave nor free, male nor female, for you are all one in Christ Jesus.' Christ was utterly without prejudice – equally comfortable with lawyers or lepers, men or women, the elderly or infants, prostitutes or priests, tax collectors or political zealots, Jews or Greeks.

There is a missionary model called the Homogeneous Principle. According to this, it is claimed that mission is most effective when you reach out to your own type or people group. This may make pragmatic sense – but it is fundamentally unbiblical. It may be that underlying it is a subtle prejudice. The fact is that prejudice is an enormous obstruction to mission and to a life of love. You cannot bring the love of God to the one you think yourself superior to. Prejudice throttles the love of God and the flow of the Spirit through us.

Recently, while the leadership of our church were away at a retreat, we felt God speak to us. We were aware of his peace and presence. In this case those present seemed unanimously to feel the weight of a burden and love for our continent of Europe. We had been sitting over dinner discussing how each of us was feeling in terms of where to direct the energy we had for mission. One after the other, those around the table spoke about a stirring for mainland Europe. Perhaps because of its history, Europe has become a barren place spiritually and we spent the evening praying and asking and dreaming of how Christian communities might grow up throughout Europe, our continent. One of the exciting things about being in the Church is that God may speak to us, and when he does, things will begin to happen. Several months later, therefore, we sat down with dozens of leaders from across the continent to consult and be together. We had been looking for our brothers and we had found some of them; and the finding was joyful.

Yet in seeking to bring a love and discover a sacrificial desire to serve French people, German people, Turkish people, we may find that we need to repent completely, and turn away from our inherent prejudices. The fact is that such prejudices have in the quite recent past led to immense warfare and bloodshed.

The year 2010 was the sixtieth anniversary of a proposal submitted by French Christian statesman Robert Schuman for the creation of a united Europe. This was a project that he claimed was indispensable for the maintenance of peace in a continent that was just emerging from half a century of carnage. Since the beginning of the twentieth century, some ninety million people had been killed in Europe as a result of war. At the end of the Second World War, Winston Churchill pleaded: 'We are asking the nations of Europe between whom rivers of blood have flowed to forget the feuds of a thousand years.'[5] There can be little doubt that what came to be known as the 'Schuman Declaration' has proved to be an astonishing success.[6] It may now be under threat economically, but Europe has prospered and enjoyed the kind of protracted peace that would have been unimaginable previously.

However, on that sixtieth anniversary, I found myself reflecting on the past and on the legacies that will be left for future generations. Schuman was a convinced Christian and his vision was rooted in Christian values. But this legacy is largely forgotten today. It seems ancient Christian boundary stones are being removed, and all over our continent there is an uprooting of the vestiges of the overwhelmingly Christian foundations of our culture. It seems likely that the tide of post-Christian legislation will continue. In this context, and the intense pressure that this brings to Christian communities, I am particularly looking for my brothers in Europe, our mission field.

Carl Jung said: 'The Christian missionary may preach the gospel to the poor naked heathen, but the spiritual heathen who populate Europe have as yet heard nothing of Christianity.' More recently, Pope Benedict has been calling on Europe not to forget her spiritual roots, saying: 'Europe is united by its culture which gives it a common identity. The roots which formed . . . this continent are those of Christianity.'

That weekend on retreat, our church, prophetically nicknamed a 'house of prayer for all nations', had an epiphany of the needs of our nearest neighbours: the countries of Europe. What was it that drew us and led us? It was ordinary circumstances. One of our team had spent the summer travelling in mainland Europe and had been gripped by the opportunities to help build the Church there. Another had returned from living in Bosnia with a story of need and opportunity. For myself, I had spent ten years in Paris serving a French church and seeing at first hand the beauty of Christ in an inner-city community which loved authentically and the influence of which thus spread like wildfire. As we shared our stories around the table, it was an epiphany of the ordinary leading us to say: yes, let us try to make a difference and be of help in our continent.

There is no doubt that Europe is a strategic place for Christians to get involved and give up their lives. The countries of Europe show ten signs which I believe highlight its status as a continent in crisis:

1   A negative birth rate.

2   A growing population of the elderly.

3   A declining workforce that cannot create sufficient wealth to sustain the commitment of the welfare state and pensions.

4   A financial crisis threatening the Eurozone and beyond, which could be catastrophic.

5   Large numbers of immigrants from former colonies and refugees from natural disasters and political upheaval, creating multi-ethnic communities with many different languages and religions: this highlights the challenge of how to bring social cohesion in the context of cultural and religious diversity when ethnic and racial prejudice is all too often alive and well.

6   Young people who are turning their backs on traditional religion to seek authentic expressions that are relevant and fulfilling. The perception of the institutional church as impersonal, remote and irrelevant.

7   A European culture deeply influenced by the Enlightenment, led by rationality and logic – our understanding of God has to conform to our human understanding and behaviour; he has to be politically correct.

8   The weighty baggage of European church history, which has skewed its witness, relevance and ability to minister effectively.

9   Staggering biblical illiteracy, where the Bible, which so richly influenced the development of European thought and civilisation, does not provide a meta-narrative or a foundational framework for public discourse.

10 A longing for God and a longing for community.[7]

I am struck by the indifference – we might call it prejudice – of so many in England to their sisters and brothers across the water in mainland Europe, the ghetto-like lack of love between Christian people. But I believe we are called to buck the trend and radically love one another. I want to be filled with the generous love of God and energetically seek for those who can join in this great adventure of loving. I believe it is a time for greater unity, partly in order to survive in a continent-wide time of darkness, but particularly because of Christ's call to 'love your neighbour as yourself'.

I believe that in Europe we are facing the collapse of Christian civilisation as we have known it. We are living in what can sometimes feel like a kind of war against faith in our land.

And yet days of darkness can be the days of greatest opportunity. In Paris, I saw a French church come to life, develop and expand before my very eyes. In the space of ten years, a group of forty became a family of four hundred. We are going to go on to look at the epiphany that happens when we see community and discover how to build it. We will see a love/hate relationship hopefully becoming a ceaseless love affair within the Church. I certainly awakened to this in a poor part of Paris. When I wrote a book on prayer I dedicated it to my beloved Parisian fellow-believers: 'I think of you – believers from Lebanon, Egypt, Israel, Morocco, Cameroon, Togo, Benin, Rwanda, Nigeria, Algeria, Congo Republic, Madagascar, Brazil, USA, Columbia, Guadeloupe, Dominican Republic, Haiti, Ireland, Portugal, Britain, Germany, Switzerland, Sweden, Norway, Austria, Russia, Iran, China, New Zealand, Philippines, and of course France. Watching you worship God together is like a foretaste of heaven.'[8] It was as if this city of Paris, one of Europe's world-class cities, had become a house of prayer for all nations – and in God's good grace, he had given us the chance to see it, to bring those peoples together. Stop and look: can you *see* it?

Collect for Europe

Lord, you cleansed your Temple and made her a house of prayer for all nations. You called us to ask of you that you would give us the nations as our inheritance. We ask you for nothing less than you have asked us: mercifully grant that the people in the nations in the entire continent of Europe come back to lively faith in you, Lord Jesus. Amen.

my love is building a building
around you,
a strong fragile house . . .
e.e. cummings, my love is building a building (XII)

On this rock, I will build my church.
Matthew 16:18

CHAPTER SEVENTEEN

Building: The bride who looks like a city

My father was an architect who restored ancient houses. Much of my time with him as a child was spent visiting old houses and halls given in trust to the nation and in need of careful restoration. We would climb up into roof spaces or down into cellars and tap the wood for dry rot, or the walls for integrity. We would wander round with what seemed (from their great age and wizened features) like a dying breed of craftsmen. Eventually, the diagnosis would be given, the treatment prescribed and the money granted. Then the house would rise up again, as if from the ashes of obscurity, to serve the country in what was sometimes a brilliantly new form, but with an evocatively recognisable beauty. Like a new wineskin to contain a new vintage, a new setting for a new population, these houses and halls were ruins restored. I remember the old Suffolk landmark Hintlesham Hall turning into a signature restaurant for the chef Robert Carrier. I remember Pembroke College turning ten seventeenth- and eighteenth-century houses back to front, negotiating the permanent closing of a road in the middle of Oxford, and inventing a completely new quadrangle as the college emerged to show the way forward for a city architecturally. When I asked my father how he did it, he said: 'You have to see it first.'

I think that where my father was an architect of buildings, I serve as an architect of a living building – the Church.

Where he restored and repaired, extended and re-envisioned buildings, I do this with the Church and with people. Where he worked with bricks and mortar, I work with flesh and blood. Where he restored beautiful buildings that will crumble in the end, I work with a structure of great but faded beauty that will survive when every other structure has gone. But we have this in common: we are both in the restoration business, for the Church is both ancient and future. It has an ancient past but is our future hope.[1]

For my father, this ancient/future challenge was a long love affair. Every journey taken in a car with him was a guided tour of Britain's buildings, informing us of dates, mistakes, cost-cutting disasters and moments of design genius in whatever buildings we passed, from council houses to court houses, from pubs to churches and everything in between. He loved them all. While I don't want to write a guide to dreams, dates, disasters and discoveries of the Church today, I do want to write of a love affair.

Maybe you have fallen in love at some point and remember the lurching changes that happen as the thought that life will never be the same again percolates through to your subconscious. For myself, I have fallen in love only three times, but three times is enough. The first was with a beautiful girl who put her arm through mine as we walked through Christ Church Meadow, Oxford. I remember when that happened, and everything changed forever.

The second time I fell in love, it was with Christ himself. He emerged from under the rubble of political correctness where my ideas as an Oxford student in the 1970s had buried him, and when I at last saw him, I loved him!

The third time I fell in love it was with a much older woman. She was classy – her family had so much history and destiny. She had a beautiful singing voice and I delighted just to sit and listen to her music, which moved me. She was a great dancer. She had a voice which was clear and true and gave me shivers of home-coming when I heard her speak. She had a wonderful perfume that intoxicated me. She lived self-lessly and served the poor. In fact she gave away her money and lived in community in a way I had never encountered before. When I met her in the city of York in the seventies, I wanted to be with her forever. I am talking about the Church, the bride of Christ, that ancient community which is the future of the world. I love her and never tire of talking of her, and believe that mankind is dying for want of finding her truths. She is the body of Christ and as such is the hope of the world. She is the extended family of the father. She is the living building that we all need to belong to and however hard it is, to get joined into.

The first time I fell in love it was with the one who later was to become my wife. Since that 'meadow moment', over thirty-five years ago, I have not stopped finding out new things about her. I am fortunate that I can truly say she still fasci-nates me. But in the same way, some thirty years on from our first encounters, both Christ and his Church continue to fascinate, beckon, intrigue and romance me. I have served the Church as a pastor for ten years in the cultural desert of an outer London county called Essex; for ten years in the artistic glory but physical poverty of inner-city Paris, building in a French-speaking context; and now for ten years in the intel-lectual greenhouse but spiritual winter of Oxford, England.

In every context, I have been ambushed. I have discovered hidden treasure in the Church of which I scarcely knew. In Essex, it was a simple love that painted an otherwise forlorn landscape with such bright colours. In Paris, it was the beauty of nations, and in Oxford, it has been her pioneering capacity to change the world.

Some people in their marriage have not had that opportunity of a long obedience in the same direction. Divorce, illness, death have exerted their pressure. Passionate monogamy seems to be becoming rare – and it is certainly under attack. Not a day passes without articles in British newspapers inspiring married couples to commit adultery, spurred by the example of high-profile celebrities and sportsmen. It has become fashionable to justify and promote the extramarital affair not just as likely but as good and healthy. We are told this is just being realistic.

Perhaps in a similar way, devotion to the Church (the bride) has been under fire. The attacks come from two different sources: enemy fire and friendly fire. I guess it is inevitable that atheists will attack the Church.[2] What is more surprising is that Christians should do so. But it has become sadly fashionable in the West for some Christians to attack, criticise and pronounce the Church as we know it to be 'finished'.

At times the 'Emerging Church' movement does this. There have been some good insights from the movement, but there are aspects that feel like friendly fire. One idea this movement promotes is that we are at a once-every-500-years historical point of shift, where a new kind of Church emerges. The old kind of Church is finished and we need to invent something entirely new. It may be true that we are at a pivotal point. But whatever the importance of this time, there risks being a battle as to what exactly will emerge.

The 'Emerging Church' movement draws on the cultural movement of postmodernism to seek fresh expressions and sometimes calls itself 'post-evangelical' and indeed 'post-charismatic'. For myself, I want to be not 'post-' but pre-charismatic and pre-evangelical, or simply biblical. I want to find a strong future expression of ancient living, as seen in the book of Acts. I want the future to be ancient, not in the 'Church Fathers' sense but in the 'Word of God' sense. I see exactly this same yearning all around the world in a movement that I want to call the 'real emerging Church'. I want to make an attempt to rekindle love and hope for the ultimate community, the Church, even though her love may at times have grown cold or even died; and I want to inspire others to join in as builders and restorers.

Across Europe, Africa, the Middle East, the Americas and Asia, we can watch the Church adjust, emerge and 'come of age' in different ways. She is not perfect, but there is what could be called a New Reformation taking place, particularly as the centre of gravity shifts to the global South. Observing the radical, intelligent, passionate leadership in the global South, I have found myself preaching in Kampala, Uganda, on the idea that 'the tail has become the head',[3] as African Christians come forward, especially in the Anglican Church, to take leadership in a way that many are now recognising.

Tim Dearborn[4] expressed it like this:

Globally, we are in the midst of a transformation of the church that is far more substantive than the Protestant Reformation. That Reformation challenged the old structures of an imperial Roman Church and theology, birthing a renewed emphasis on justification by faith and releasing the laity to lead the church. Since then, the Roman Catholic Church has gone through wonderful renewal and remained strong. The new Protestant structures thrived and have experienced both renewal and atrophy. Today, we are seeing a similar but even more dramatic change. The old structure of the imperial Western evangelical movement continues but is waning. The center of Christendom has shifted to the South. This church bears marks that are transforming world Christianity, including that in the West. We stand in the midst of the intersection between the old and the new. Will Western evangelicalism allow itself to be transformed by these changes, or will it atrophy?

In his observation of the Church that is emerging, Dearborn speaks of:

• Worship as a dramatic encounter with the power of God, rather than a passive and comforting moment of education and encouragement.
• Community as a gathering of people rather than a cluster of programmes and activities.
• Mission as a daily encounter with the demonic and evil, conducted through spiritual battle, suffering and a holistic engagement with the world; for all of life is deemed as the domain of God, with social, economic and even political ministry integral to church life.

Dearborn is an observer of the Church in the global South. As such, he may have a better understanding of the real 'Emerging Church' than those viewing only an American or European postmodern culture. But where can we go to find an epiphany that will help us in knowing which kind of Church will emerge in the end? As usual, a good place to look is in the Bible.

Epiphany: a bride who looks like buildings
One of the most mysterious moments in that book of epiphanies called the book of Revelation comes in chapter 21

where John writes: 'I saw the Holy City, the new Jerusalem, coming down out of heaven from God, prepared as a bride beautifully dressed for her husband.' How a bride can look like a city is left to our imagination, but evidently she can. One might think that heaven should rather look like a garden or at least a landscape unspoiled by human constructions – but apparently not. Heaven is a city. We get a glimpse of community and a huge number of people living together with enough room for all. The space is well designed, harmonious and filled with light. Equally surprisingly, not only is heaven a city-bride, but she is to be Jerusalem herself. In 4,000 years of human struggles so far, Jerusalem has been a packed jumble of cacophony and chaos, history and havoc. It has seen golden times of glory, but has also stoned the prophets, and turned to idolatry and indulged in the worst rebellions. But here, Jerusalem descends, perfect, redeemed onto the earth. The wreckage left by Absalom's rebellions, Nebuchadnezzar's invasions and modern conflicts has all been redeemed. All things have been made new.

Looking at some of the detail, we see:

> the Holy City, Jerusalem, coming down out of heaven from God. It shone with the glory of God, and its brilliance was like that of a very precious jewel, like a jasper, clear as crystal. It had a great, high wall with twelve gates, and with twelve angels at the gates. On the gates were written the names of the twelve tribes of Israel . . . The wall of the city had twelve foundations, and on them were the names of the twelve apostles of the Lamb.[5]

Note that what is in heaven is coming down. It is an invasion of the perfect future into present reality. It is not that we are leaving earth, but that heaven is joining or coming down to earth. This has implications for our care of the planet and the sacredness of stuff on earth. It may be that a new heaven and a new earth is created, but this happens because heaven comes down. N.T. Wright speaks of the implications of this for different semi-heresies around:

> The great claim of Revelation 21 and 22 is that heaven and earth will finally be united. This is the polar opposite of all kinds of Gnosticism with their ultimate separation of heaven and earth . . . eventually heaven and earth will be impregnated with each other . . . God's heaven, God's life, God's dimension impregnating, charging the present world, eventually producing new or renewed heavens and new or renewed earth integrated with each other . . .[6]

It is worth noting that the names of the twelve tribes and the twelve apostles are written into the gates and the foundations of the city. All of the tribes were unfaithful, and at times went to war with each other. But now they are transformed. Similarly, the apostles were all too human. They argued, and they all fled at the arrest of Jesus. Some were obscure and have slipped almost forgotten from view. Peterson remarks that five of the apostles are more or less story-less: 'James son of Alphaeus, Bartholomew, Thaddeaus, Simon the Canannean, and Matthias, who replaced Judas Iscariot. By the last decade of the century when St John's Asian Christians were leaving home, taking up their crosses and following their Lord, half the apostolic names . . . were sunk into unremembered obscurity. [Yet] all twelve were part of the foundations of the city.'[7] All of this shows that God uses, affirms, promotes and rescues the obscure, the forgotten and the disappeared. He redeems, remakes and restores the failed and the forlorn as his new and beautiful city-bride appears like ancient buildings made new.

Another distinctive feature of this epiphany is the jewel-quality colour:

> The wall was made of jasper, and the city of pure gold, as pure as glass. The foundations of the city walls were decorated with every kind of precious stone. The first foundation was jasper, the second sapphire, the third chalcedony, the fourth emerald, the fifth sardonyx, the sixth carnelian, the seventh chrysolite, the eighth beryl, the ninth topaz, the tenth chrysoprase, the eleventh jacinth, and the twelfth amethyst. The twelve gates were twelve pearls, each gate made of a single pearl. The great street of the city was of pure gold, like transparent glass.[8]

Analysing these colours is complex but breathtaking. So there is green jade, blue lapis lazuli, misty white jade, emerald-green jade, pale grey/pink sardonyx, red sard, honey-gold quartz, sea-green amazonite, yellow-green topaz, apple-green chrysoprase, lavender jade, purple-violet amethyst. It is anything but dull: the glory of God's brilliant creation comes down to earth in the form of a bride of many colours, nations, tribes, and ends up gloriously beautiful. Like Joseph the dreamer with his richly ornamented robe, it is as if this is a dream of multicultural, multicoloured community come down to earth.

The other features of the bride-who-looks-like-buildings are light and openness, purity and harmony. One day, God's Church-bride will be like this. At present, there is a lot of darkness. We walk through the valley of the shadow of death for too much of the time. We can come across shameful and deceitful activities, in the Church as much as outside it. Community is flawed. One day it is glorious, another it is hideous. In this arena we can be tempted to give up, to call the endeavour a failure.

But what this epiphany at the end of the Bible does is to prepare us to persevere. It lifts up our eyes to a future hope. It gives us a vision of heaven. If we have no vision we may either perish or cast off restraint. So this unveiling of glory stops us being monochrome and dulled. When he paints his sunflowers, a painter like Van Gogh helps us to see yellow in a way we have never seen it before. Mondrian may give us an experience of line and pure colour we have never seen.[9] When we look up to God in worship, colour and beauty and delight can and should invade our world. The choice to worship daily is to glimpse eternity, colour, glory, beauty. It is a choice to see heaven open, to be re-envisioned and to be re-energised; to be involved in Jesus' building of his Church on earth.

Rob Bell's first book (on the Church) puts it like this:

She's a mystery, isn't she? Still going after all this time. After the Crusades and the Inquisition and Christian cable television. Still going. And there continue to be people like me who believe she is one of the best ideas ever. In spite of all the ways she has veered off track. In spite of all the people who have actually turned away from God because of what they experienced in church. I am starting to realise why: The church is like a double-edged sword. When it's good, when it's on, when it's right, it's like nothing on earth. A group of people committed to selflessly serving and loving the world around them? Great. But when it's bad, all that potential gets turned the other way. From the highest of highs to the lowest of lows. Sometimes in the same week. Sometimes in the same day.

This analysis describes the tension we live with: the Church is bad news for too much of the time; but nonetheless, it remains the best news there is. God is in the business of redemption – and he never gives up. Bell goes on:

> But she will live on. She's indestructible. When she dies in one part of the world, she explodes in another. She's global. She's universal. She's everywhere. And while she's fragile, she's going to endure. In every generation there will be those who see her beauty and give their lives to see her shine. Jesus said the gates of hell will not prevail against her. That's strong language. And it's true. She will continue to roll across the ages, serving and giving and connecting people with God and each other. And people will abuse her and manipulate her and try to control her, but they'll pass on. And she will keep going.[10]

The last feature to mention of this vision is fruitfulness and fecundity.

> Then the angel showed me the river of the water of life, as clear as crystal, flowing from the throne of God and of the Lamb down the middle of the great street of the city. On each side of the river stood the tree of life, bearing twelve crops of fruit, yielding its fruit every month. And the leaves of the tree are for the healing of the nations. No longer will there be any curse. The throne of God and of the Lamb will be in the city, and his servants will serve him. They will see his face, and his name will be on their foreheads. There will

be no more night. They will not need the light of a lamp or
the light of the sun, for the Lord God will give them light.[11]

The destiny of the Church is to be a place of fruitfulness:
every month there is to be a crop of fruit within this bride-
who-looks-like-a-city. It is as we work, live and do life
together that fruits of the Spirit come to birth: love, joy,
peace, patience, kindness, goodness, faithfulness gentleness
and self-control are the nine fruits from Galatians. In my
experience, three other fruits needed in the Church are:
forgiveness, faith and thankfulness. I would like to encourage
you to set out on a year's discipline of bearing one fruit per
month – ask God for one of these twelve each month for a
year, as a prophetic sign of what is to come.

The vision also speaks of the healing of nations. The
Church can learn from this to bring to birth an international
emphasis in our communities. For some of us this will require
repentance and a change of heart. I have already referred to a
theory propounded by Donald McGavran and Peter Wagner
called the 'homogeneous unit principle' (HUP).[12] According
to this theory, churches with one homogeneous social stratum
attending will grow well; others, which seek to reach several
different people groups, may find it more difficult. While
there may be truth in this, it is in fact neither a biblical nor a
truthful sign of what is real in church life. I found this out in
a cross-cultural context. When I moved to Paris, I discovered
I would be living in a district where it seemed you changed
continent every ten metres. In a walk down the cosmopoli-
tan, poor and ragged Rue de Belleville, the shops pronounced
they hailed from China, then North Africa, then Israel, then
Poland, but they were hardly ever French. I had to unlearn
the HUP and invest in building something different, and it

was this revelation that helped me see what I believe Christ has in his sights: the Church for all nations. Church without barriers – an *Eglise sans frontières*. It is a Church whose 'leaves . . . are for the healing of the nations'.

How this is needed today. One of the joys I have in my work is facilitating this honouring of nations. So in France we would have at times the *repas des nations* (All Nations Feast). This meant an evening of incredible food prepared to celebrate the best of all the influences we had within the church. Usually, dancing and celebration followed. I remember a hilarious procession around the room with paper napkins held aloft and some African worship song being sung at the tops of voices by all. I remember Norway marrying the Lebanon – ice and fire – and the floor-bashing Norwegian wedding dances that stamped their imprint unforgettably on our community. It is true that in a foreign country, sometimes one can be freer culturally than at home, but back in my own country, in Oxford, I have seen similar things: a hilarious Brazilian night, a celebration of China, as well as fun-filled Thanksgiving dinners to celebrate what we affectionately call our former colony, the USA.

At different times we have had in our Oxford church, among our staff and spouses, a Muslim-background Ugandan, a South African, two Americans, two Polish, three French, an Austrian, two Chinese and one Irish, to say nothing of several Brits, and one Zimbabwean seconded to us. I think this is an advantage: I encourage it. First, because it prepares us for heaven – where every tribe and tongue will gather round the throne of God. If this is what is to come, it is good to get used to it in advance. Second, it is a biblical pattern. Already in the church at Antioch in Acts 13, there were different nations and colours in the leadership team. Third, I think that people from other countries bring fresh eyes and often more faith than those who grew up under European skies. So a multicultural team will help us be the Church in our city.

This is one more reason I love, serve and believe in the Church. May she continue to mature and grow and emerge from the desert 'leaning'. To jump back to the inspired words of Song of Songs for a moment – 'Who is this coming up from the desert like a column of smoke, perfumed with myrrh and incense made from all the spices of the merchant?' May it be the Church for all nations, bringing with her an aroma that has to be smelled to be believed!

Collect for Building
Lord Jesus, you taught us in your Word to build our house upon the Rock. Mercifully grant that we might be used of you to participate as expert builders, taking care how we build, that the Church throughout the world may be joined together and rise to become a holy temple in the Lord. Amen.

Let nothing disturb thee
Nothing afright thee;
All things are passing;
God never changeth.
Patient endurance
Attaineth to all things;
Who God possesseth
In nothing is wanting;
Alone God sufficeth.
Teresa of Avila

I believe in Kingdom Come
Then all the colours will bleed into one . . .
But I still haven't found what I'm looking for.
U2, 'I Still Haven't Found What I'm Looking For'

Lord you may now dismiss your servant in peace . . .
For my eyes have seen.
Luke 2:29

CHAPTER EIGHTEEN

Departing

I remember ringing my father from a ferry on our way back to France to tell him that I had applied for and been appointed to the post of Rector of St Aldates in Oxford. His reaction was memorable: 'St Aldates?' Then he sighed and said quietly: '*Nunc dimittis servum tuum, Domine . . . in pace.*' He was quoting Simeon's prayer when Jesus was first brought to the Temple, in effect saying: 'Now I can die happy.' I think it may have been partly because after our years apparently lost among the poor in France, this was at least a 'proper job'! But maybe it was more because he had been the architect for Pembroke College next door and had become acquainted with the reach and influence into the lives of Oxford students and future leaders, as well as the poor, of this wonderful church we now serve.

At any rate, once I had understood what he was saying, I reacted by telling him he was nowhere near 'departing' and I expected to see him present at my induction in Oxford. Sadly, as it turned out, in the nine months between the idea of moving and the reality of arriving, the shadow of his death did fall, and he never lived to welcome us home.

That conversation has been in the back of my mind when over the years I have meditated on Simeon's 'departing in peace'. Now, at the end of this book, it is fitting to turn to the subject of 'finishing well', the task of persevering, after the different epiphanies that may come our way, through to the end, whenever that may come.

The fact is that many 'heroes of faith' in the Bible, for all their wonderful achievements, do not finish well. If we think of David or Solomon or Gideon, or even godly young Josiah, whose life finished prematurely because he 'did not listen to the words of Neco from the mouth of God',[1] we see that departing in right standing with God is a challenge.

Perhaps this is truer today than at any other time. People live longer, and endure greater physical weakness, so remaining faithful to holy dreams and to God for a lifetime is challenging on a new level. It seems that almost weekly we read of people who 'fall' morally and spiritually, often well after their sixtieth birthday. Whether it is politicians, sports administrators, journalists, business leaders, educationalists, it seems like a syndrome. And Christian leaders are not exempt. Whether it is the stress of office, pressure of life, or a moment's carelessness or recklessness, people fall. So to see Simeon and Anna 'waiting for the consolation' and still living powerful prophetic lives into their eighties is a fine encouragement with which to end this book.

Simeon's sighting is redolent with significance, as was that of the Magi with which we began our journey. It happens forty days after the birthday of Christ, when the time comes for the Presentation of Jesus in the Temple, sometimes known as Mary's 'Purification', celebrated annually on 2 February.

I sometimes ask myself how often dear Simeon wondered if he had waited in vain, like so many of us. We read that he was 'looking for the consolation of Israel'[2] and that he had been told he would not die before he saw the Lord's Christ. At any rate Simeon, moved by the Spirit, went into the Temple courts. He was in the right place at the right time.

And when the parents brought in the child, as the law required, everything made sense. It was an ordinary moment, a bit like registering a birth. But in his being there, and seeing salvation, Simeon's whole life made sense.

As I draw this book to a close, I return to the image of new fathers or mothers holding their child in their arms for the first time. I have listened to the stories of so many: they are often aware of an epiphany. Sometimes people will say they had no idea of the existence and depth of the wells of love within them that the arrival of their own child draws forth. As I have said: this is an epiphany of love. We need to treasure and look after this well of love. It will not, God willing, run dry, despite the times of trauma that come to every family. The same may be true of grandparents, whose wellsprings of love are renewed and replenished as they hold a grandchild in their arms for the first time. They are awed by the power of love. Parents and grandparents alike may be struck by the risk and vulnerability this brings as they embark on a lifetime of care and affection for a new human being who up until then they had not met. Yet the child triggers into being a crowd of emotions.

What of those who are childless? Will the arrival of a baby not remind them of their own longing or loss? But even those who are single can find themselves arrested by love as they welcome a new child of a friend or relative, like Anna who came up after Simeon and rejoiced at the birth.

I think of Anna as one who was perhaps childless. We know she had suffered the loss of her husband early in life. And yet she rejoiced unreservedly. What was Anna's story? We read: 'She was very old; she had lived with her husband seven years after her marriage, and then was a widow until she was eighty-four.'[3] She had, no doubt, a secret history. I would love to have heard it.

I am reminded of the story of one single woman approaching her forties and childless. She had every year deeply dreaded and often completely avoided Mother's Day services at church because of the conflicting emotions, sadness and loss that were dragged up in her in spite of herself. Yet one year, reading Isaiah's 'Sing, O barren woman' passage, a journey of gathering wisdom, of new insight, began. It came to completion at the arrival of a child to whom she was to be godmother. Then she too had an epiphany.

She 'heard' God say to her: Sing, O barren woman, you who never bore a child; burst into song, shout for joy, you who were never in labour; because more are the children of the desolate woman than of her who has a husband.[4]

It was as if, gradually, she came to understand the privilege of being a single person who could extend love to dozens of children and enjoy them all. A bit like Heidi Baker in Mozambique,[5] one called to be a 'mother to many', she saw her own destiny in the ordinary event of the birth of another person's child. And her life was transformed from one of bitter sorrow to a beautiful spreading out of love. From now on she would give herself to these children. She would make time for them. She would be an aunt to many in a world so in need of extended families. For this one woman, that moment of epiphany signalled the beginning of a journey to healing.

Returning to Anna: she stands, I believe, for the many senior people in our communities. They are worth getting to know, and worth hearing. In an age of obsession with youth, and neglect of the elderly, we need to be reminded of this. In our church community in Oxford, we meet in extended family groups we call 'pastorates'. One of these was successful partly because it was a real mixture of people in their twenties and thirties alongside the elderly. Last summer, Anita and I visited the dilapidated country house that this group books for a week each summer and saw the connections between old and young. We saw the affection, community and respect between the generations. In this day of collapsing culture and disintegrating community, the Church can connect the generations perhaps like no other people on earth.

So Anna loved him and Simeon took him in his arms. This is a moment of tenderness and affection, of love for Christ after long years of waiting. It is a moment of joy and peace. It is a moment to savour and, I believe, one that is common to many who at last *see*! Simeon breaks out in a glorious love poem, the Nunc Dimittis,[6] translated here in the King James Version: 'Lord, now lettest thou thy servant depart in peace, according to thy word. For mine eyes have seen thy salvation, which thou hast prepared before the face of all people; a light to lighten the Gentiles, and the glory of thy people Israel.'[7]

It is interesting that this happens at the end of his life. Simeon is old. Rembrandt's paintings of the Presentation show him as achingly so, and seemingly almost sightless. And yet at almost the last moment of his life, he sees this wondrous thing.

The same is true of Simeon's counterpart, Anna. She is eighty-four years old, but she too is waiting – waiting for epiphany; as Luke puts it, for the redemption of Israel. Again, they have had an inkling of what is coming; they are waiting and preparing and praying, and then they see it.

The epiphany happened late in life. If you are reading this at age sixty, perhaps this means that you have only twenty-four years still to wait for destiny to arrive, if it is to be at the same age as Anna! Things that are mighty can happen when we are old, and we can finish well. It was not until he was seventy-five that the saintly John Stott was eventually named by *Time* magazine as 'one of the 100 most influential people on earth'.[8]

And in our time there are thousands certainly who are similarly preparing and praying and waiting. They are doing their best to be in the right place at the right time, so that they might see his glory, and finish their lives lovingly and well. Perhaps there are those who may want to pause, to remember promises of old for them or for humankind. It may be the promise of revival, the promise of renewal for a child, the promise of awakening for a country or a community. Today's Annas and Simeons may be those called to a lifetime of loving prayer and waiting, as well as pouring out love, until he comes. Perhaps those reading who identify with this will be encouraged to dust off their dreams and reignite them in the place of prayer so that they are in the right place at the right time – so that they are 'in the Spirit on the Lord's Day', as John on Patmos was, so that at last they may see it and depart in peace.

Here is an old man, Simeon, seeing at last what he has dreamt of for years. And now, he says, he can depart in peace: to use the vernacular, he can 'die happy'.

We may ask: What is it that can enable man, born to die, to use such language as this and to say he can 'depart in peace'? What can take the sting of death away? There is really only one answer to this: a sight of Christ and his power; faith in Jesus to take away our alienation and lostness and sins, and reconcile us to God.

This is an experience common to all, at whatever age, who see and understand who Jesus is. Simeon sees this in a moment of epiphany. One old saint who used to preach once a year in the church I serve comments on this:

What can deliver from the fear of death? Nothing but strong faith can do it. Faith laying firm hold on a Saviour – faith and faith only can enable a man to look death in the face and say: 'I depart in peace'. It is not enough to be weary of pain and sickness and ready to submit to anything for the sake of a change. It is not enough to feel indifferent to the world when we have no more strength to enjoy its pleasures. We must have something more than this if we desire to depart in real peace. We must have faith like old Simeon, even that faith which is the gift of God. But dying without such faith we shall never find ourselves at home when we wake up in another world.[9]

Many reading this, having learnt how to see, may be comforted in the face of death. And if not, why not reach out and lay hold of him now and put your trust completely in Christ, like old Simeon? May we all have our energies renewed by the example of Anna and Simeon and be able to 'finish well'; and, at the end of our journey, short or long, depart in peace, having seen our salvation.

Cranmer's First Evening Collect
O God, from whom all holy desires, all good counsels, and all just works do proceed, give unto thy servants that peace which the world cannot give, that both our hearts may be set to obey thy commandments and also that by thee we, being defended from the fear of our enemies, may pass our time in rest and quietness; through the merits of Jesus Christ our Saviour. Amen.

'Come,' he replied, 'and you will see.' So they went and saw where he was staying, and spent that day with him. It was about the tenth hour . . .

'Come and see,' said Philip . . .

'You shall see greater things than that . . . you shall see heaven open, and the angels of God ascending and descending on the Son of Man.'
John 1: 39, 46, 50

Epilogue

Come and see

Right at the start of John's Gospel, Jesus invites two disciples who ask where he is staying to 'come and see'. They go and spend the day with him and their lives are changed forever. Philip is named as one of them, but the other has no name. I like to think this is because each one of us can identify with the unnamed disciple and be invited to 'come and see'. We are all at some point called to leave the search for power, wealth and reputation that our culture promotes, and dwell with Christ.

Abide

As the disciples spend the day with Jesus, we are not told what they talked about. It is their 'secret history'. Jean Vanier reflects: 'We all have our secret meeting with God, with truth, a "peak moment" that has touched and opened our hearts to God. I can imagine that these two men, while they "dwelt" with Jesus were enveloped in an immense inner peace.'[1] What we do see is that these two remained with him all day, they found out what it was to 'abide' with him. As I discover this, I want each day not to disturb or jolt away his loving presence, but learn to rest in his healing love.

Go

Simon and Andrew's epiphany is so compelling to their souls that they can't help passing the news on. They 'go', in this case to Nathanael. When Jesus tells Nathanael he has already seen him under the fig tree, he instantly believes. What was it that was so momentous to him that the discovery that Jesus knew about it immediately brought him to become a disciple? We don't know, but are told that Nathanael will see greater things than that.

This book has been about some of those greater things that Nathanael was promised. We are at the end of our journey. But the epiphanies explored in this book speak across the centuries to us, calling us to keep alert. They call us to watch out and to know the times in which we live. They call us to 'look up!', to watch for the Holy Spirit, to watch out for the consolation of Israel which will surely come. The kings of the original epiphany saw his star in the East and came to worship him. After that life-changing encounter, they could go home satisfied. And so may we. As John the Baptist and John on Patmos saw their respective visions of God's purposes, they could know that their mission was not in vain; indeed, in bearing witness to Christ, it was accomplished. And as Simeon and Anna saw those purposes revealed in Christ, so they went and 'spoke about it to all who were looking for the redemption of Jerusalem'.

'Go forth and set the world on fire.' said Ignatius. May we, having seen his glory, and having learnt to abide in him, go out to do the same.

Cranmer's Second Evening Collect
Lighten our darkness, we beseech thee, O Lord, and by thy great mercy defend us from all perils and dangers of this night, for the love of thine only Son our Saviour Jesus Christ. Amen.

Notes

Chapter 1

1 From 'A Defence of Heraldry', in *The Defendant, Essays published in The Speaker* (1901).
2 Anonymous, *The Cloud of Unknowing* (Penguin Classics, 2002), p. 12.
3 Psalm 63
4 2 Chronicles 7
5 Ezekiel 1:4–5
6 Ezekiel 1:22–26
7 Ezekiel 1:27
8 Ezekiel 1:28
9 Daniel 1:20
10 Daniel 7:9
11 Daniel 7:10
12 Daniel 7:13–14
13 James Joyce, *Stephen Hero* (Jonathan Cape, 1944).
14 All the stories that follow are well documented in many different sources. See, for example, Hugh Thomson Kerr and John M. Mulder, *Famous Conversions: the Christian Experience* (Eerdmans, 1983).
15 John 1:14
16 See Luke 9:28–36.
17 2 Peter 1:16–18

18 A.W. Tozer, *God Tells the Man Who Cares* (Authentic Publishing, 1994), p.19.

19 Thomas Merton, 'The Wisdom of the Desert', in Henri J.M. Nouwen, *The Way of the Heart* (HarperCollins, 2009).

20 Luke 9:28–29

21 See Matthew 17 and Mark 9.

22 1 Timothy 6:15–16

23 Luke 9:29–31

24 Revelation 5

25 Dietrich Bonhoeffer, *Life Together* (SCM Press, 1972), p. 75.

26 Matthew 3:17

27 Henri J.M. Nouwen, *In the Name of Jesus: Reflections on Christian Leadership* (Crossroad Publishing, 1989), p. 37.

28 Mark 9:7

29 John 17:24–26

Chapter 2

1 Douglas Coupland, *Life After God* (Simon & Schuster, 1994), p. 359.

2 C. S. Lewis, *The Magician's Nephew* (Lions, 1990), p. 144.

3 The earliest reference to the feast in the Eastern Church is a remark by St Clement of Alexandria. Today in Eastern Orthodox churches, the emphasis at this feast is on the shining forth and revelation of Jesus Christ as the Messiah and second person of the Trinity at the time of his baptism. It is also celebrated because, according to tradition, the baptism of Jesus in the River Jordan by John the Baptist marked one of only two occasions when all three persons of the Trinity manifested themselves simultaneously to

humanity: God the Father by speaking through the clouds, God the Son being baptised in the river, and God the Holy Spirit in the shape of a dove descending from heaven – the other occasion being the transfiguration.

4 John 1:29–31

5 John 1:32–34

6 Luke 7:19–23

7 Luke 7:27–28

8 This and subsequent quotes are taken from an interview by Peter Stanford with Tony Jordan for *The Daily Telegraph*, 18 December 2010.

Chapter 3

1 Exceptions might be Esther and Jude. Even in Jude we have references to struggles between angels and to 'standing in the presence of his glory'.

2 Leviticus 9:23

3 Saint Augustine, *The Trinity* (New City Press Edition, 1991), p.116.

4 A.W. Tozer, *The Pursuit of God* (Authentic Publishing, 2004), p. 21.

5 Exodus 33:7–11

6 Exodus 33:13–18

7 Exodus 34:5–7

8 See Psalm 31:21: 'Praise be to the LORD, for he showed his wonderful love to me when I was in a besieged city.' And Psalm 103:17–18, 'But from everlasting to everlasting the LORD's love is with those who fear him, and his righteousness with their children's children – with those who keep his covenant . . .'

9 Song of Songs 1:2; 2:4

10 See Matthew 3 and Luke 3.

Chapter 4

1 Revelation 1:13–16

2 'The lion has roared – who will not fear? The Sovereign LORD has spoken – who can but prophesy?, (Amos 3:8).

3 Eugene Peterson, *Reversed Thunder: The Revelation of John and the Praying Imagination* (HarperSanFrancisco, 1991), p. 37.

4 Hebrews 4:12

5 John 1:4–5

6 Nouwen, *In the name of Jesus* (Crossroad, 1989), p. 42.

7 See Peterson, *Reversed Thunder*, for more.

Chapter 5

1 John of the Cross, quoted in the *Catechism of the Catholic Church* (Burns & Oates Ltd, 2002), p. 231.

2 C.S. Lewis, *The Four Loves* (Harvest Books, 1960), p. 3.

3 In an extension to C.S. Lewis's 'Moral Argument for the Existence of God', some would say that the existence of 'Love' on planet Earth is a proof of the existence of God, the source of Love. See, for example, C.S. Lewis, *Mere Christianity* (Macmillan, 1952); Art Lindley, *Love, the Ultimate Apologetic* (IVP, 2008).

4 T.S. Eliot, *Murder in the Cathedral* (Harcourt Brace, 1935).

5 A.W. Tozer, *The Pursuit of God* (Authentic Publishing, 2004), p. 21.

6 Luke 10:27

7 John 21:15–17

8 Revelation 1:9

9 See Revelation 2.

10 Exodus 34:6ff.

Chapter 6

1 Nouwen, *In the Name of Jesus*, p. 37.

2 Richard Rohr, *The Naked Now: Learning to See as the Mystics See* (Crossroad Publishing Co., 2009), p. 38.

3 *A Further Account of God's Dealings with the Reverend George Whitefield*, originally 1747, www.quintapress. com/files/whitefield/Journals.pdf

4 From his sermon in December 1843: 'The Revelation of God's Glory'; see http://www.gospeltruth.net

5 Referred to in Richard Foster, *Prayer: Finding the Heart's True Home* (Hodder & Stoughton, 1992).

6 'It is called Recollection because the soul collects together all the faculties and enters within itself to be with God.' From Saint Teresa of Avila, *The Way of Perfection* (Cosimo Inc., 2007), p. 160.

7 In Foster, *Prayer*, p. 172.

8 J. Hudson Taylor, *Union and Communion* (China Inland Mission, 1914).

9 In Foster, *Prayer*, p. 168.

10 ibid., p. 169.

11 Raimon Panikkar's *The Experience of God: Icons of the Mystery* (Fortress Press, 2006), pp. 12–13.

12 Matthew 14:27

Part II
Chapter 7

1 From the sermon 'Love to Jesus', delivered 30 September 1860, by C. H. Spurgeon at Exeter Hall, Strand.

2 Psalm 23:2

3 Richard St Victor (d. 1173), 'Explication of the Song of Songs', in *The Church's Bible*, ed. R.L. Wilken (Eerdmans, 2003), p. 212.

4 John of Ford (1150–1214), 'Sermons on the Final Verses of the Song of Songs', in *The Church's Bible*, ed. R.L. Wilken (Eerdmans, 2003), p. 217.

5 Apponius (c. seventh century) in *The Church's Bible*, ed. R.L. Wilken (Eerdmans, 2003), p. 218.

6 Mark 10:21

7 The great Scottish divine John Owen thought that the Song of Songs was 'totally sublime, spiritual, mystical' and strongly commended James Durham's commentary, *The Song of Solomon* (Banner of Truth, 1982), p. 305.

8 See John 17; Romans 8.

9 Mike Bickle, *Song of Songs – The Ravished Heart of God, Part 2* (Friends of the Bridegroom, 1995), p. 31.

10 Song of Songs 4:9

11 Bernard Ramm in Nicky Gumbel, *Questions of Life* (Alpha International, 1999), p. 35.

12 ibid., p. 310.

Chapter 8

1 Song of Songs 1:2

2 Origen in *The Church's Bible*, ed. R.L. Wilken (Eerdmans, 2003), p. 21.

3 'Here Is Love', words by William Rees, music by Robert Lowry (1876).

4 Durham, *Song of Solomon*, p. 74.

5 James Pennington, *The Song of Songs* (SLP, 2004), p. 15.

6 Bernard de Clairvaux, in *The Church's Bible*, ed. R.L. Wilken (Eerdmans, 2003), p. 23.

7 C.H. Spurgeon, *The Most Holy Place* (Christian Focus, 1996), p. 70.

8 Taylor, *Union and Communion*.

9 Herman Hesse, *Narcissus and Goldmund* (Noonday Press, 1988).

10 Charles Finney, (ed. Robert Backhouse), *The Classics on Revival* (Hodder & Stoughton, 1996), p. 249.

11 George Marsden, *Jonathan Edwards: A Life* (Yale University Press, 2003), p. 245.

12 Richard Sibbes, Vol. 3, *A Discovery of the Near, Dear Love, Union and Communion Betwixt Christ and His Church* (Ogle and Hamilton, 1809), p. 3.

13 Samuel Rutherford, *Letters* (also known as *Joshua Redivivus*), (Portage Publications, 2007). Available to download from http://www.portagepub.com/products/caa/sr-letters.html

14 Attributed to Henry Finck.

15 P.B. Shelley, from *Prometheus Unbound* (1818–19), The Moon, Act IV, I. 145.

16 Attributed to Carrie Latet.

17 Song of Songs 1:2–3

18 Luke 1:15

19 2 Corinthians 2:14–15

20 'Thy Name is like Ointment Poured Forth' http://www.hymnal.net/hymn.php/h/1084

21 Gregory the Great in *The Church's Bible*, ed. R.L. Wilken (Eerdmans, 2003), p. 33.

22 Nilus of Ancyra, in *The Church's Bible*, ed. R.L. Wilken (Eerdmans, 2003), p. 73.

23 See Song of Songs 2:7; 3:5; 8:4.

24 Durham, *Song of Solomon*, p. 133.

Chapter 9

1 Matthew 24:12

2 From a sermon given by C.H. Spurgeon at the Metropolitan

Tabernacle, Newington, in 1865 on Song of Songs 1:7, from the *Modernized Edition of Spurgeon's Sermons*, ed. Larry and Marion Pierce (Winterbourne, 2010).

3 Wm Paul Young, *The Shack* (Hodder Windblown, 2008).

4 Song of Songs 2:10–13

5 Matthew 24:9–12

6 St John of the Cross, 'The Dark Night', from *The Collected Works of St John of the Cross*, trans. Kieran Kavanaugh and Otilio Rodriguez (ICS Publications, 1991).

7 Song of Songs 3:1–4

8 ibid., 5:7

9 Luke 6:26

10 Song of Songs 5:10

11 From his article in *The Times*, March 2010.

12 Song of Songs 3:6

13 Ambrose of Milan, ed. R.L. Wilken, *The Church's Bibles*, (Eerdmans, 2003), p. 149.

14 Luke 21: 25–26, 28

15 Song of Songs 8:6–7

Chapter 10

1 Psalm 91:1

2 Carol Arnott, *The Purpose of Soaking in His Love* (Spread the Fire, Summer 2001).

3 Psalm 91:2–3

4 Psalm 94:18–19

5 Psalm 119:81, 97

6 John Wesley's famous 'Aldersgate Experience' was on 24 May 1738. See, for example, Frederick A. Dreyer, *The Genesis of Methodism* (Lehigh University Press, 1999), p. 27.

7 John Wesley, 'Preface to Sermons 1–53' (Christian Classics Ethereal Library), www.ccel.org

8 1 John 3:16

9 Charlie Cleverly, *The Passion that Shapes Nations* (Victor, 2005).

10 *Selected Writings of Hugh Latimer*, selected and ed. Arthur Pollard (Fyfield Books, 2000).

11 'Safe in the Arms of Jesus', words by Fanny Crosby and music by W. Howard Doane (1868).

12 John 3:16

13 From Henry Drummond, *The Greatest Thing in the World and Other Addresses* (FQ Classics, 2008) p. 8.

14 Psalm 91:15

15 See Mike Bickle, *The Pleasures of Loving God* (Charisma House, 2000), p. 74, for more on this subject.

16 Luke 21:28

17 Isaiah 50:4

18 Luke 1:76–79

Chapter 11

1 Song of Songs 1:6

2 http://www.landmarkforum.com

3 For more on this story, see Anita Cleverly, *Destiny's Children* (Kingsway Publications, 2005), p. 2.

4 Myers-Briggs type indicators are a combination of qualities, for example ESTJ: extroversion (E), sensing (S), thinking (T), judgment (J); or INFP: introversion (I), intuition (N), feeling (F), perception (P).

5 Henri J.M. Nouwen, *Sabbatical Journey* (Crossroad Publications, 1998), p. 100.

6 This and following quote: Song of Songs 2:14–15.

7 Song of Songs 2:16–17

8 John 17:26

9 1 John 4:19

10 Ephesians 3:19

11 C.S. Lewis, *Surprised by Joy* (Harvest Books, 1955).

12 See Romans 8.

13 See Revelation 2:1–7 as a parallel passage to Ephesians 1:3–14.

Chapter 12

1 From T.S. Eliot, 'Little Gidding', in *Complete Poems and Plays* (Faber & Faber, 1969), p. 283.

2 'He stood praying, being full of the grace of God for full two hours, so that he ceased not for full two hours.' John Foxe, *The Book of Martyrs* (London, 1824), p. 43.

3 ad. Fratres Sermon 22.

4 John Piper, *The Legacy of Sovereign Joy: God's Triumphant Grace in the Lives of Augustine, Luther, and Calvin* (Crossway Books, 2000), esp. pp. 106ff.

5 See Pete Greig, *Red Moon Rising* (Kingsway Publications, 2004) and Pete Greig and Andy Freeman, *Punk Monk: New Monasticism and the Ancient Art of Breathing* (Regal Books, 2007).

6 This phenomenon is charted particularly by Pete Greig in the book of the movement, *Red Moon Rising*.

7 Mike Bickle's International House of Prayer in Kansas City is one most hopeful sign of life inspiring a generation.

8 See http://www.oxfordprayerroom.org for more information.

9 Paul Hattaway, *Back to Jerusalem* (Authentic Media, 2005) or see http://www.btj.org.uk

10 E.M. Bounds, *A Treasury of Prayer* (Whitaker House, 1997), p. 71.

11 John 15:7–8

12 John 15:16

13 I have a photocopy of the *Daily Express* of 7 June 1944 publishing this appeal.

14 James 4:1–3

15 2 Kings 2:15

16 Matthew 28:20

17 John 17:24

18 Luke 8:7

19 Tozer, *God Tells the Man Who Cares,* p. 9.

20 Cleverly, *The Discipline of Intimacy* (Kingsway, 2009). Available from St Aldates Church, www.staldates.org.uk

21 See Cleverly, *Discipline of Intimacy*, for remarks on the prayer life of Abraham, Esther, Hannah, Joel, Isaiah, Habakkuk, Jesus and Paul.

22 Exodus 32:24

23 Exodus 33:7–18: 'Now Moses used to take a tent and pitch it outside the camp some distance away, calling it the tent of meeting . . . As Moses went into the tent, the pillar of cloud would come down and stay at the entrance, while the LORD spoke with Moses . . . Moses said to the LORD, ". . . teach me your ways so I may know you . . . Remember that this nation is your people . . . If your Presence does not go with us, do not send us up from here . . ." Then Moses said, "Now show me your glory."'

24 Daniel 32:11

25 Those wishing to study a 'theology of nations' see Genesis 12, Joel 3, Matthew 28:19, Acts 17:26.

26 Psalm 127:1

27 Psalm 133 *KJV*

28 John 17:24

Part III

Chapter 13

1 Matthew 25:40

2 From an explanation of the Original Constitution in *Mother Teresa – The Private Writings of the Saint of Calcutta*, ed. Brian Kolodiejchuk (Doubleday, 2007), p. 41.

3 ibid. p. 41.

4 Malcolm Muggeridge, 'Me and Myself' in *Jesus Rediscovered* (New York: Pyramid Publications, 1969), p. 157. Originally printed in *The Observer*, 15 December 1968.

5 Quinquagessima is the Sunday fifty days before Easter.

Chapter 14

1 John 15:13

2 Matthew 11:11

3 Luke 1:15

4 Mark 6:20

5 See 1 Kings 17 and 18.

6 Daniel 3:17–18

7 See Acts 6 and 7.

8 See John Foxe, *Martyrs*, for this account of Archbishop Thomas Cranmer's death.

9 Bonhoeffer, *The Cost of Discipleship* (SCM, 1959), p. 79. See also his books *Ethics* (Fortress Press, 2008) and *Life Together* (Fortress Press, 2004).

10 Bonhoeffer, *Discipleship*, p. 79.

11 1 Corinthians 13:3

12 For more on this distinction see Charlie Cleverly, *The Passion*, ch. 2: 'Martyrdom or Suicide?'.

13 Ephesians 5:25

14 Matthew 20:26

15 *Cry from Iran* DVD available from Open Doors: http://www.opendoors.org

16 Name and location removed from this and following example to protect the people and work going on there.

17 Elliot Tepper's 'Betel' network of churches working among and rescuing drug addicts serves as a particularly shining example of greater love. See http://www.betel.org and http://www.betel.org.uk

18 The story of Captain Chavasse and excerpts from the letters quoted here can be found at: http://www. chavasse.u-net.com/chavasse.html

19 This famous quote is from Winston Churchill's speech to the House of Commons, 20 August 1940.

20 Churchill, speech given 18 June 1940.

21 Martin Luther King's famous 'I have a dream' speech was given on the steps of the Lincoln Memorial on 28 August 1963 to over 200,000 civil rights campaigners who had come together for the 'March on Washington for jobs and freedom'.

22 From King's 'I've been to the mountain-top' address at a rally on 3 April 1968 at Mason Temple, in Memphis, Tennessee.

23 From Mandela's statement from the dock at the opening of his trial on charges of sabotage, Supreme Court of South Africa, Pretoria, 20 April 1964.

24 From Mother Teresa's Nobel Lecture, 11 December 1979.

Chapter 15

1 1 Samuel 16:18
2 1 Samuel 17:28
3 John 7:4–5
4 Jude 1:24

5 Douglas Coupland, *All Families Are Psychotic* (Flamingo, 2001).

6 Douglas Coupland, *Life After God* (Simon and Schuster, 1994), p. 250.

7 Matthew 5:45

8 Revelation 2:4–5: 'Yet I hold this against you: You have forsaken your first love. Remember the height from which you have fallen! Repent and do the things you did at first.'

9 Psalm 133:1–3

10 Matthew 12:48–49

11 Acts 2:42, 47

12 See www.loveoxford.org.uk for more information on Love Oxford.

Chapter 16

1 Acts 10:11–20

2 See Acts 10:28

3 Charlotte Brontë, *Jane Eyre* (Penguin, 2006).

4 Jane Austen, *Pride and Prejudice* (Wordsworth Ltd, Reprint, 1992).

5 From Churchill's 'Ambition for Europe' broadcast, 14 February 1948.

6 The Schuman Declaration can be found at: http://www. eurotreaties.com/schuman.pdf

7 I am grateful to George Kovoor, Principal of Trinity College, Bristol, for inspiring this list.

8 Charlie Cleverly, *Intimacy*, p. 8.

Chapter 17

1 This Ancient Future idea was coined first by Augustine then popularised by Robert Webber in several books – for

example, *Ancient Future Faith: Rethinking Evangelicalism for a Postmodern World* (Baker Academic, 1999).

2 There are some notable exceptions: in the *Sunday Times,* 27 December 2008, Matthew Parris wrote: 'Now a confirmed atheist, I've become convinced of the enormous contribution that Christian evangelism makes in Africa: sharply distinct from the work of secular NGOs, government projects and international aid efforts. These alone will not do. Education and training alone will not do. In Africa Christianity changes people's hearts. It brings a spiritual transformation. The rebirth is real. The change is good.'

3 Deuteronomy 28:13

4 Dr Tim Dearborn serves as Director of Faith and Development Programmes for World Vision International.

5 Revelation 21:10–14

6 N.T. Wright, *New Heavens, New Earth – The Biblical Picture of Christian Hope* (Grove Books Ltd, 1999).

7 Eugene Peterson, *Reversed Thunder* (HarperSanFrancisco, 1991), p. 176.

8 Revelation 21:18–21

9 See Peterson, op. cit., p. 178.

10 Rob Bell, *Velvet Elvis, Repainting the Christian Faith* (Zondervan, 2006), p. 172.

11 Revelation 22:1–5

12 Donald McGavran wrote that the homogeneous unit is simply a section of society in which all the members have some characteristics in common. Thus a homogeneous unit (or HU, as it was called in church growth jargon) might be a political unit or sub-unit, the characteristic in common being that all the members live within certain geographical confines. He went on to say that 'the

homogeneous unit is an elastic concept, its meaning depending on the context in which it is used. However, it is a most useful tool for understanding church growth.' More on this can be found in Donald McGavran and Peter Wagner, *Understanding Church Growth* (rev. edn., Eerdmans, 1980), p. 96.

Chapter 18

1 2 Chronicles 35:22
2 Luke 2:25
3 Luke 2:36
4 Isaiah 54:1. See also www.singbarrenwoman.com
5 Heidi Baker is the founder of Iris Ministries. She and her husband Roland have devoted themselves to helping orphaned and abandoned children in Mozambique.
6 From the Latin for 'Now Let Depart . . .'.
7 Luke 2:29–32
8 John Stott, CBE, was an English Christian leader who was Rector of All Souls and Founder of the Langham Trust. He was one of the principal authors of the Lausanne Covenant in 1974.
9 J.C. Ryle, *Expository Thoughts on Luke*, Vol. 1 (Banner of Truth, 2006), p. 67.

Epilogue

1 Jean Vanier, *Drawn into the Mystery of Jesus through the Gospel of John* (DLT, 2004), p. 41.

Do you wish this wasn't the end?
Are you hungry for more great teaching, inspiring
testimonies, ideas to challenge your faith?

Join us at www.hodderfaith.com, follow us on Twitter
or find us on Facebook to make sure you get the latest from
your favourite authors.

Including interviews, videos, articles, competitions
and opportunities to tell us just what you thought about
our latest releases.